Butterfly

A Literary Journey of Genes and Memes
through Generations

LESLEY ANNE CHRISTIAN

All correspondence to the author
Email: lesleychristian069@gmail.com

© Copyright Lesley Anne Christian

First Printed 2025

The right of Lesley Anne Christian to be identified as the author of this work has been asserted by her in accordance with the Copyright, Designs and Patents act. All rights reserved. No part of this publication may be reproduced, stored in or introduced into a retrieval system, or transmitted, in any form, or by any means (electronic, mechanical, photocopying, recording or otherwise) without the prior written permission of the publisher. Any person who does any unauthorised act in relation to this publication may be liable to criminal prosecution and civil claims for damages.

This book is sold subject to the condition that it shall not, by way of trade or otherwise, be lent, re-sold, hired out, or otherwise circulated without the publisher's prior consent in any form of binding or cover other than that in which it is published and without a similar condition including this condition being imposed on the subsequent purchaser.

ISBN: 978-0-646-71506-3

Proudly produced by

TheBookStudio
www.thebookstudio.com.au

*Many thanks to Sue Swales for the Butterfly artwork
and the rest of the Namba Writers' Collective:
Alannah McFadzean, Kathy Hickson and the great Rob Swales
for their support and encouragement to never give up.*

The fictional story, 'Searching for Rosa', includes events and characters based on knowledge gleaned from personal relationships with my family members during their lifetime and those clearly in the public domain. Any resemblance to real persons, living or dead, is purely coincidental. Timelines, ages and dates of events and characterisations are fictional.

As to factual events and characterisations, these are based on ancestral sources and from various academic resources employed in completing my Creative Writing Artefact for my Masters in Creative Writing. A bibliography formed part of my Exegesis and Artefact.

I acknowledge and pay my respects to the past and present Traditional Owners and Custodians of Country throughout Australia and recognise the continuation of culture, spiritual and educational practices of Aboriginal and Torres Strait Islander peoples.

In regard to factual dates and events involving Aboriginals in Tasmania, I relied upon the work of Nicholas Clements in *The Black War*, first published 2014 by University of Queensland Press.

'Metamorphosis' is my story.

Lesley Anne Christian BA.LLB, M Com

For my daughter
My desire
My inspiration

Where do I come from? Where did you find me? asks the baby of the mother.
She weeps and laughs at the same time and pressing the infant to her breast, answers,
You were hidden in my heart, darling, you were its desire.

- **Rabindranath Tagore** -

Life is mostly froth and bubble
Two things stand like stone
Kindness in another's trouble
Courage in your own.

- **Adam Lindsay Gordon** -

Searching for Rosa

PROLOGUE

I am the butterfly who, with elegance and grace, flits from flower to flower, mind to mind, seeking out the nectar, the stories, which lie dormant, awaiting discovery, to be supped upon and if found tasty, to be spread throughout a dry, thirsty, curious world. I am not the noisy bumble bee that threatens innocents with its sting should they, per chance, cross its path on their own journey. Possessing superior colour vision I am able to sense more wavelengths than the humble bumble bee or those humans who, out of fear of loss, strike out at others. I can see the colour red. The bee cannot. I do not fear variations of colour. On the contrary, they attract me. I am a gatherer of stories not a hunter of bounty. Consequently, I am considered by some as a second class pollinator because of my fragile nature. I admit to being vulnerable to changes in my environment, but my strength lies in my pupa, the chrysalis. I have the ability, through metamorphosis, to change, to transform. Just before I emerge as an adult, ready to feed the world with nectar, the chrysalis becomes transparent. The next generation can be viewed through this translucent film. As often occurs in nature, upon giving birth, its purpose having been fulfilled, the nurturer is abandoned to its fate, but the beauty of the butterfly and its creations continue through time.

So please join me as I inhabit my brave female ancestors' bodies, feel their pain and their joy, do what they do, see what they see and become their voice. Like nectar, their stories will spread, becoming part of the world's story, as it should be.

Fragments of a Life

I have a dream, or is it memory? From above, as I descend, I see squalor. As I enter the warmth of a body I look down. I see a squirming mass of legs and arms some black, some white, some grey, like a nest of vipers. I start to cry, it is the cry of the newborn. I feel the pain of embryonic lungs as they take their first breath. Something clings to me. My eyes cannot distinguish who or what it is. All I see is movement. Another cry rises from the depths of this indignity. Born of one who lies there cast adrift like a trapped fish caught in a snag of tangled line, of no further use, cut loose, discarded, never to be known, but present all the same both in 1829 and thereafter in the lives of her descendants.

Rose

Pondicherry. Southern India

It is 1834. I am five years old today. The sun is low. Only its glow rises above the houses. The city of Pondicherry, Southern India is quiet. There is no rhythm, no music until the conductor taps his baton, the sun rises and the harmony begins. My Papa sits by my bed. He is gently welcoming me to the morning.

'Bon anniversaire mon petit pétale de rose.' He leans down to kiss me on the cheek. His whiskers tickle me wide awake. Squirming through bearded snuggling, I push my way through to gasp air and freedom from love.

'Come back,' he protests, 'I have a gift for you.'

I don't heed his request, I run down the hall through the pantry and out into the garden.

I call her name, 'Rasna. Happy birthday, Rasna.'

A small brown hand draws open the scarlet curtain of purdah. The familiar percussion of bells and trinkets which adorn her swaying sari accords her presence. Those big black eyes tell me nothing. Is she happy or sad today?

I say, 'I love you, Rasna' and she responds with a smile that starts at the corners of her mouth and travels in my direction. She jumps up and runs towards me. Her little pink tongue points the way. I grab her hand as big sisters do and drag her into the house.

'Presents,' I exclaim. Without the need for further explanation we both explode into the parlour where the presents await. Papa hugs us both and requires us to sit down and '*comportez vous comme des jeune filles.*' '*Oui docteur*', we say in unison as we run past him and like ravenous beasts tear apart the pink cherubs suspended on a sea of blue wrapping paper. My gift is a music box. When I lift the lid, the beautiful Taglioni dances *en pointe* to the music of *Giselle* as her pink tutu rotates to the beat.

Rasna carefully unwraps her precious trophy of love. She finds a pair of pink ballet slippers and a pink tutu. A gasp of joy. She looks towards the kitchen door. Banita's wise eyes observe the emotion. She decides to encourage Rasna's joy by lifting her hands to her heart as one does in prayer and supplication.

'Aunty, look, it is such a lovely gown. Look at the slippers. I am a ballerina too.'

'Papa,' I say, 'we three will dance for you tonight, you will have three ballerinas, Rose, Rasna and *Giselle.*'

'*Bien*. I will look forward to the performance.' He goes to the hall stand, puts on his white coat and places the stethoscope in the right hand pocket and heads towards the door. Rasna runs after him, grabbing at his coat, 'Your bag Papa, the one made of dead pigs, aren't you going to take it today?'

'*Non ma petite*' he says, 'I don't need it today.'

'Who told you my bag was made of dead pigs?'

'Oh silly old Tai told me, Papa.'

Papa looks to the heavens, 'Well, it seems I must once again speak to that old reprobate.'

I watch as Papa returns to the hall stand. I watch as he stares into the mirror. He strokes his 'foreign' nose. I remember *Grand-mére* telling me that Papa's British friend at University, Charles, would say Papa's nose was contrived by a committee who couldn't see eye to eye. Upon hearing this, *Grand-mére* would demand that Papa not be offended by his classic features – 'that *garçon* is only *jaloux* of your *beaute*, pay no heed to him, you have a wealth of nose my son,' at which point Papa would respond, '*oui Maman*, I am blessed with an over-abundance of nose.' They would both laugh.

I run up to him, 'I love your nose, Papa.'

He looks down and smiles, 'I love your nose too, Rose – it is just like Papa's, but don't worry you will grow into it *ma cherie.*'

Aunty Banita is directing us away from Papa so he can escape our version of domestic bliss.

'Farewell, Doctor Sahib Aachie Aziz' she says and Rasna and I chime in with our usual farewell song, *'Adieu Docteur Papa Aziz'*.

Fragments of a Life

Through my sensitive proboscis I experience a difference in perspective. I jump the narrow hiatus between two minds. I have a dream, or is it memory? As I enter the warmth of a body I look down to see my source of life, silent and still, at the mouth of a raging river of red. I cry out in response to another who has voiced their presence. They share my existence and my loss. I cling to them. I am not alone.

Rasna
Pondicherry. Southern India

It is 1834. I am Rasna. I am five years old. My Papa says my name Rasna in Hindi means *'tongue.'* He says I have a beautiful tongue. I enjoy poking it out and making people laugh. It is pink, my favourite colour. My beautiful tutu and ballet slippers are pink. They were a present from Papa on my birthday. Papa sat in the big red chair and watched Rose and I dance to the music in the box, up on our toes, like *Giselle*. Aunty Banita helped us dress and watched from the kitchen door. As I danced around I kept on looking at Papa to see if he was watching me or Rose. I would then look at Aunty Banita. She always looked at me. She is like my mother. My mother died when I was born. She is my mother's sister. She tells me how beautiful my mother was. She tells me I am like my mother, beautiful on the inside and on the outside. I know Aunty loves me. She loves Rose too but Rose sleeps in Papa's house while I sleep in Aunty Banita's house. When I ask why this is so she says it is just the way it must be. I don't understand. I am Papa's daughter too but I look like Aunty Banita, not like Papa, not like Rose. Old Tai says I am like him, Indian. Papa says I am the best of both races, French and Indian. I don't understand but he smiles when he says this and I love Papa and I trust him, so it must be right.

I know *Grand-mére* loves me but one day I heard her say to someone, 'Yes, Rasna is beautiful but you should see Rose she is truly beautiful she looks just like me and her Papa.'

Pondicherry. Southern India

It is 1839. I awaken to my tenth birthday. As I lie in bed, I can hear my *Grand-mére* Madame Rosemarie De La More, shouting as usual, about something the British have done '*qui n'a aucune logique.*'

'They have no understanding of the Indian.'

'Why don't they….' starts off most of what she has to say these days. Today it is why don't they, the British, work with the French to help India?

Her voice reaches a crescendo.

'The British have never forgiven us for taking Clive prisoner at Fort George.'

Papa tries to calm her down. '*Maman*, that was a long time ago. Britain and France are no longer at war. What happened then is not relevant to the problems India faces now.' He tries to explain to her that it is more about the dependency of India on the British. The days of being self-sufficient ended with the closure of India's home spun cotton industry and the cloth factories. The industrial revolution in England was at the heart of this loss.

His voice falters as he concludes, 'Millions of Indians have been left without any means of support. India is at the beginning of a push for independence. It is resentful of foreigners but fearful of a future without them.'

'I know,' she says, 'But we French are as vulnerable as the British. As Europeans, we are identified as the enemies of India. Again, I ask, why did you save those children? You should have left them lying where they dropped in Black Town. Two Eurasian girls in India. They will never survive. You must leave and leave now.'

'*S'il te plait Maman*, lower your voice. Don't start on that nonsense again. You know I could not let my daughters die. Their mother's life and tragic death was enough of a sacrifice. As their father, I have a moral responsibility. We are on the brink of a new India. I can provide them with a future. They are being educated through the schools established by the French. As you well know, my beloved father, by providing me with the opportunity to study medicine, has 'bequeathed' to me the value of an education. It is my duty to my children and their children to do the same. As an educated Indian, my father was able to help his people. Like his friend Ram Mohan Roy, India's freedom fighter has shown, independence flows from independent thinking which flows from education. The British know that they cannot put that particular genie back in the bottle. The same will happen with our women. The British have outlawed Sati – no more Hindu widows will burn on the funeral pyres of their dead husbands.'

'*Mais, mon cher garçon* do you not see how the Indians look at you and your daughters as you walk the streets. You are also despised along with the British. All foreigners are the enemy now. I warn you, I know you think I am a silly old woman, but you will see, one silly mistake by the British and you and your precious daughters will be in danger too. Being French will not save you. You should return to France.'

I lean over to my music box beside my bed. I lift the lid, the music begins, *Giselle* dances, and the conflict is silenced.

Papa comes into my room and sits by the bed. '*Bon jour*

mon petite pétale de rose, let me brush away those tears from your beautiful rose coloured cheeks, it is your birthday – there will be no tears today.'

'Papa, why is *Grand-mére* so angry?'

'Well', he says, 'There are a lot of angry people in India at the moment.' Just then Rasna comes in and jumps on the bed.

Papa welcomes her with happy birthday hugs and kisses.

'Go on Papa,' I say, 'Please explain to us why everyone is so angry.'

He tries to explain. It is about a house and who is going to tell the people who live in the house what they can and cannot do in their own house. Some of the people who live in the house don't like the rules and they start smashing up the furniture and hurting the people who made the rules.

'What will happen, Papa?'

'Nothing bad will happen to you, *mes cherie*, in this house we follow Papa's rules. We love one another, are kind and respectful of all those we come in contact with. We are safe in this house.'

Rasna hugs Papa, 'But Papa, old Tai says you and Rose and *Grand-mere* will leave India and I will be left here alone.'

'That will never happen, Rasna.'

We cling together on that tiny bed, as if shipwrecked, waiting for rescue.

Rasna
Pondicherry. Southern India

It is 1839. It is my tenth birthday. I run into the house and find Papa and Rose looking serious as usual. I jump in between them. They can't help but laugh. Papa tries to grab my tongue as usual as I purposely poke out its pinkness at him. After acknowledging my birthday with hugs and kisses, Papa gets serious again. He tells this story about a house and people who break the table and chairs. Aunty Banita's house doesn't have a table and chairs so I don't understand why this is something to worry about. Old Tai gets serious with Aunty Banita sometimes. I heard him tell her that Papa and *Grand-mére* and Rose will go away and I will be left behind. Papa says that will never happen. I love Papa. I believe him.

Fragments of a Life

Guilt or innocence? I watch with sadness and horror. Justice is not sought in London at the beginning of the 19th century. The goal is to solve a problem. The problem is the poor, the homeless, the men, women and children who have had to resort to begging, stealing and murder to survive. Transportation to the other side of the world is the solution. Out of sight out of mind. They will become someone else's problem. Some would argue transportation is cloaked in altruism. It is providing the circumstances consistent with the building of a new society in a new country. It is providing a new start for the hopeless. Others see an alternative motivation, that cloaked in commercial terms, the opportunity to create new trade, to fill the pockets of the already rich and of course, boost the power of the British Empire. There is no sentimentality, no grace, no kindness.

I hover above one of these unfortunates. As I enter her body my sensitive proboscis experiences her pain and suffering just as the chrysalis is breached and she welcomes new life into a harsh, cruel planet, inhabited by harsh cruel people who have had no experience of grace and kindness. Will she and her children survive? Will they be capable of building a kind and graceful society?

Number 53
Hobart Town. Van Diemen's Land

It is January 1829. I am a fifteen year old female. Identifying characteristics read: 'face and breasts freckled, scar over left eyebrow' and behaviour during the voyage is described as 'guilty of pregnancy, useless, malingerer.' It is four o'clock in the morning as we are herded off *The Harmony*, the vessel that has transported us, some 100 women and 33 children from London to Van Diemen's Land. The early hour is to avoid trouble with the men of the colony who have been starved of female company.

There was little harmony on board over the six month

journey. Many babies and mothers died. I have survived and so has this unborn child I carry.

I have been transported here because I stole a gentleman's pocket watch. He weren't no gentleman, as it turned out. I tried to tell the Judge that I had agreed to lie with the gentleman in return for money for food. I says, 'Judge, I ain't got no ma or pa, I ain't had no schooling and I ain't got no work.' I got to eat, ain't I? Then I tells him 'after he had his way with me, the gentleman, he done turned his back on me and don't pay what he owes me.' I don't tell the old beak I followed the gentleman and picked his watch from his pocket. I was unlucky, someone saw me and the police grabbed me. 'Guilty – caught in the act,' says the Judge, 'Transportation to Van Diemen's land for seven years.'

I was three months gone when I left London. Now, as I get bogged in the muddy Macquarie Road, I know I will have me baby soon. I do not expect either of us to survive. Death will be a welcome release from this miserable life. I saw women as they died during childbirth on the voyage. Once not of this world, their bodies had found peace. They no longer hurt.

A scream rises from a woman who has watched another walk into a spider's web trapping her like a fly. The sticky film refuses to detach itself. The spider is searching through her hair for escape. A guard grabs her pushing her forward along the path. I stumble as I catch sight of a two headed animal which bounds towards us, its huge tail propelling it forward.

Mary, who has been like the mother I never had, helps me back up on me feet. She whispers, 'Be brave for your child'. I stagger on. The guard leading the way points ahead to a stone wall and big steel gates. 'Come on you useless lot,' he laughs, 'Welcome to our newest hotel, Hobart Town's Female Factory. You are its first overseas guests.'

We are put into lines, stripped and scrubbed with caustic carbolic soap, and in a final indignity, our heads are shaved. I cry as me auburn curls collect around me feet like dead snakes. I go into labour. No sympathy is afforded, or expected. I am shuffled into a small room called the hospital. I am left alone. I am afraid. I scream in pain. A man, a surgeon, he says, enters the room. He makes me lie down and he pushes me bent legs towards me head. I lose consciousness. I re-enter the world to the screams of a newborn. 'It's not over yet' says the surgeon 'there is another child on the way, my girl'. Me babies are taken away. I am dressed in a rough shift which is intended to cause discomfort and does. Eventually the babies are brought to me to feed. They are wrapped in thick coarse blankets. They are placed on me bulging breasts. I find the suckling agony. I scream out. A nurse enters the room and says, 'if you can't feed them there is no one else to feed them so if you want them to survive you will bear the pain.' They survive and so do I. Apparently me only god given talent is survival. After three months the babies are weaned and taken to an orphanage. I am no longer a human with a name. I am a number. Me babies are also given numbers but I have secretly named them. I whisper to them as the guard comes to take them away, 'Ma will find you and steal you away.'

In the weeks that follow I cannot eat and I am labelled a trouble maker. I am placed in the cells for the obstinate and unruly. I am let out for an hour each day. Today I start to yell and scream and receive a whipping from the overseer. Mary is there. She leans down towards me as I lay spread eagled on the cobble stones, blood flowing from a cut on my forehead. 'Girlie,' she whispers to me, 'If you want to get your babies back you have to follow the rules. You must behave. If you do, you will be assigned to a free settler as a domestic. You will be free of this place. You will be able to find your babies.'

I follow the rules. I reach the assignment list. The settlers are due today. We are herded through showers of freezing water. We stand in line like beasts of burden being assessed for suitability. The overseer reads out our statistics. Age, temperament, physical and mental defects, skills. He stands before me.

'Number 53. 16 years old. Scar above left eye brow. Pock marking on cheeks. Teeth missing. Auburn hair. Blue eyes. Irish. Fertile. Behaviour of late has been conformist. She is compliant. She can cook and clean and her personal hygiene is excellent.'

A man with a huge belly grabs me shoulder-length locks pulling me head back as he forces me jaws apart so he can inspect me teeth. He asks me to turn around. I comply. There is a tap on me shoulder and I am pushed forward. I become part of a line of girls selected. We are herded inside where we are provided with appropriate attire. I dress in the bloomers and the skirt and blouse made of finer fabric than I am used to. The knitted red shawl I wrap around me shoulders. A small white cap is thrust upon me head. I am handed a bag with personal hygiene items and an apron. A horse and cart stands waiting. I climb up next to me employer. He whips the horse and we are off. I am free of the Female Factory but not yet free to regain me babies. I yell above the noise of horses hoofs on the gravel road 'Me name's Sarah'.

Rose

Pondicherry. Southern India

It is 1844. I am 15 years old. Papa says I am becoming quite the educated *jeune fille*. I have been studying Indian history at school and Papa and I have interesting discussions on political and social issues. I have learned that the abolition of slavery came late to India. The Slavery Abolition Act was enacted in 1833 in the United Kingdom. However, it excluded territories in the possession of the East India Company.

Ram Mohan Roy, India's religious and social conscience, worked tirelessly for this exclusion to be removed. He used his influence to bring social justice to Indians. In particular, he lobbied for the removal of the Sati and Hindi laws of ancestral disposal of property which adversely affected Indian women. He appealed to the Christian populace through his newspapers and direct communication with religious leaders to secure aid for famine-smitten natives in Southern India.

It is the 7th April 1843. This is a red letter day in the Aziz household. Papa has arranged a party to celebrate the removal of the exclusion of slavery in India. Aunty Banita and Rasna, who now live in the house, have been busy preparing food for the party. Old Tai continues to live at the bottom of the garden. It is a relief to all as he is guilty of avoiding bathing. Papa says some people go on hunger strikes to make a point but old Tai chooses a bathing strike and the only victims are those who have to abide the smell. Tai seems to flourish from the lack of water. However, he does, from time to time, go down to the river to fish and wades in to retrieve his catch.

We gather together in the garden as Papa reads the laws that have passed.

"No Native of the said Territories nor any natural-born subject of His Majesty's resident therein, shall, by reason only of his religion, place of birth, descent, colour or any of them be disabled from holding any Place, Office or Employment under the said Company."

Papa looks around the audience. There seems little understanding evident from its constraint. Papa's *'foreign'* nose is spreading across his face as an abundance of white teeth erupts in laughter.

'My dear friends, this is wonderful. Let me go on.' He reads:

"Interests of Native subjects are to be consulted in preference to those of Europeans whenever the two come into competition – the laws ought to be adapted rather to the feelings and habits of the Natives than those of the Europeans."

A loud cheer, initiated by Tai, rises into the stillness of the Pondicherry night. The guests look up as rockets of colour fill the sky. They dance around, holding hands and singing. Musicians grab their instruments. Carnatic voices in the Teluguare dialect compete with the veena's strings which sing of love and the tambura's drone and the tavil's drumming dictate the beat. Aunty Banita and her helpers appear with food for the guests. The sweet smell of hot curries, herbs and rice fill the joyful space and satisfy the empty stomachs of the celebrants.

After the guests have gone home, *Grand-mére* calls us inside to say a prayer. Papa, Rasna, Aunty Banita and I, bow our heads and pray for India. Papa and *Grand-mére*, who knew Ram Mohan Roy, thank him for leading the country. The significance of the day is lost to most of the celebrants but we trust Papa, if he thinks the news is good, then the news is good.

The next day at school, our Professor, who has studied in England and France, considers that, at the very least, the new law will set a standard which will give the independence movement something to aspire to. We study in detail Ram Mohan Roy's views on the plight of women in India. He used logic to counter the views of the proponents of Sati law and the Hindi laws of succession based on the inferiority of the female. He argued that, in many ways women were superior to men in virtue, trustworthiness, and control of their passions. He argued that if you fail to provide the female with the opportunities afforded men then you cannot in justice pronounce on their inferiority.

Our Professor points to the real issue – who should be responsible for the widows and children?

Rasna

Pondicherry. Southern India

It is 1844. I am fifteen years old. Aunty Banita and I have been in purdah this week because we bleed. Tonight we can join in the celebration arranged by Papa. Tai has even had a bath in the river. Papa reads out the words important to India. Cheers rise from the celebrants when he finishes speaking. We eat food prepared by Aunty Banita and *Grand-mére*. After the guests have gone home Papa, *Grand-mére* and Rose and I bow our heads, close our eyes and thank Ram Roy Mohan for helping India. The next day at School our Professor is also very happy. I am glad that widows don't have to be burned with their dead husbands. Our Professor says there have to be changes to the laws to protect the widows.

I ask, 'who will look after the widows if they do not have husbands?' Our Professor says that women will be able to work, earn money and look after themselves and their children. They will be able to own a house. I like that idea. I smile. I will live in a house like Papa's house with my Aunty Banita and Tai provided he promises to have a bath every day.

Fragments of a Life

Sorrow fills me. I have restrained my intrusion of my beloved during their grief. I had welcomed the promise of a new life but it was not to be. I wipe away my tears and rejoin my brave ones left to carry on with heavy hearts.

Rasna
Pondicherry. Southern India

It is 1859. I am 28 years old. Yesterday I gave birth to my first child, a boy, Aarchie Aziz – named in honour of my father. The child did not survive the birth and now resides with his Grandfather in heaven. The cord that nurtured him whilst in my womb was the viper, grey and pulsating, that choked the life out of him during childbirth. Attempts to help him breathe were in vain. I held him and told him I loved him and always would. For the first time, I saw my husband cry. James' British reserve crumbled at the sight of his 'small soldier' as he called him while he was in my belly, lying there silent and still.

James had been part of the rescue force sent from Allahabad to evacuate those under siege at Cawnpore. My dear Papa, *Grand-mére* and Rose were in Cawnpore at the time of the siege having travelled there to treat those affected by an outbreak of cholera. As the British forces approached Cawnpore 120 British women and children, including, it would seem Papa, *Grand-mére* and Rose, were captured by the sepoy forces. The reports are that they were hacked to death and dismembered with meat cleavers. Their remains were thrown down a well. This attempt to hide the evidence of the massacre failed. When the British forces recaptured Cawnpore they discovered the bodies. Outraged, the British forces themselves engaged in widespread retaliatory acts of barbarism against the captured rebel Indian soldiers and civilians. I was safe in Allahabad having travelled there to be with my husband on his first deployment with the British forces.

Grand-mére's constant warning that the British failure to respect the religion of the Indians would put all Europeans at risk had come to pass. Early in 1857 the British provided Enfield rifles to the Hindu soldiers. The cartridges were smeared with animal fat and lard. The sepoys were told to bite off the tip of the cartridge before inserting it into the open breech. They saw this as a plot to defile them and force their conversion to Christianity. At gunpoint they were ordered to load their rifles but the sepoys just stripped off their insignia and walked home to their villages. On the 9th

May, at Meerut, 85 sepoys were manacled and shackled in irons by blacksmiths and thrown into prison cells. While the British officers were in Church, the prisoners were freed and several officers were killed. The sepoys headed for Delhi. The Palace and the populace were liberated from British control two days later. The native revolt then spread to Cawnpore. In retribution, for the slaying of their women and children, the British attacked passive villagers and unarmed Indians, even faithful domestic servants were murdered.

When captured, the mutineers were strapped to cannons and blown up. Entire villages were put to the torch for the crime of proximity to Cawnpore. The legacy of the war has been that all rights of the East India Company are to be transferred to the British Crown.

Fragments of a Life

I am experiencing more pain. The loss of a mother and a sister. The loss of someone who cares for you. The loss of trust in others leading to the hatred of others. Can the young deal with such confusion and lack of wisdom?

Mary. No.55
Launceston. Tasmania

My name is Mary. I was carer for Daniel, the son of convict 53 whose name was Sarah. He was born in the Female Factory in Hobart. He was given the name Daniel by his mother. His name was written on his shirt by me. He is not just a number like his mum thanks to me. I was given the responsibility to care for Daniel after his mother Sarah was selected by a Settler. She whispered the children's names as she was dragged away. Daniel called me mummy 'til the day he left me. I was like a mother to him. I fed him and played with him. I used to tell him about his mother and his twin sister. His sister's name is Mary Rose. I didn't see Mary Rose after she left for the orphanage. Daniel has never known his sister. When he turned three, he was sent to the boys' orphanage. I remember that day. I was crying as he was dragged from my arms. The matron pushed me to the ground. 'Don't be so stupid. He's not your kid. You never had any - you're just a barren old bitch, you are not good for anything.' Daniel struggled to get free and he ran to help me dear little boy. I told him 'Go. Leave me.' I hugged him. 'Be good Daniel if you be good, your mummy will find you Daniel.' At the orphanage he was with a lot of boys like him. Always cold in that place. Cold water and beatings is what they got. Hunger too. They were sent out into the fields to plant seeds and care for the vegetables. It was a cruel place. I pray he survived that place and somehow was reunited with his mother and sister.

On the grape vine I learned Daniel and two other boys escaped when they were thirteen. They have been living rough. They made it to Launceston. They went onto a property one night and stole a horse. His friend Jimmy could ride so the three of them climbed up on the old draught horse in the middle of the night. They hid in the forest. They travelled at night. The nights would be so scary. The sound of the devils fighting and seeing the red glow of their eyes would be terrifying but compared to where they came from life on the road was safer. The locals gave them food. They lived by their wits. The people in Launceston were an easy pick. They were kind and trusting of boys like Daniel. Drinking and thieving became their life. Sadly, they have become the feared ones.

Rasna
Coonoor. South West India

My husband has retired from the Army and has now taken up a position as Inspector of Police in Coonoor. We will leave as soon as I am fit to travel but first, we must bury our beloved son. We have stayed in my Papa's house pending the birth. Old Tai and Aunty Banita have tended to my every need. They will accompany us to Coonoor. A bungalow awaits us there.

The British Constabulary's role in Southern India is not merely to maintain law and order but to also provide humanitarian assistance for the poor within the populace. A Police Officer's wife must assist her husband in this regard. I am looking forward to my involvement with the poor. I studied the Humanities in England. That is where I met my husband James. He was training to be a member of the British Forces in India. Upon my return to India, I was actively involved in the drafting of legislation for the advancement of women. My Professors at school had highlighted the need for law reform to help raise the status of women. My Papa had many friends involved in Indian politics. They encouraged me to speak on behalf of Indian women.

Rose followed a different path. Through Papa's tutelage she became qualified to treat patients as his apothecary. She ran a successful outlet for herbal remedies and medicines at the local Bazaar in Pondicherry.

Grand-mére having been a nurse in Paris in her youth, was always available to assist in midwifery. When called upon to assist those at Cawnpore, they did not hesitate. It seems they paid the ultimate price.

I stand, supported by my dear husband, at the grave of our son Aarchie Aziz. I place a bunch of wildflowers on the small white coffin as it is lowered into the dark damp earth. I do not want to leave my child alone without his mother but it will not be possible for regular visits to him so I tell him I will think of him every day and will talk to him so he should listen for my voice. I tell him I will speak through the angel who sits above his grave. Finally I tell him 'We will meet again in heaven.' As we leave the graveyard the first of the monsoonal rains drench us. A small group attends Papa's house.

Our son's life was short but memorable. I visit his grave prior to leaving for Coonoor. The headstone is in place. The small white marble angel looks down on Aarchie Aziz Brownlee. The epitaph reads:

We wanted you to stay but God needed you in heaven. Taken on July 27, 1857.

As I lean forward to brush away leaves which cover the tomb the little angel's face smiles down at me. It has lost its white marble pallor. Its cheeks are pink and alive. It is Rose. She speaks to my heart. '*Your dear son is here with me in heaven. I will keep him safe.*' I gasp as James helps me to my feet. I cannot speak. I do not know that this is only the first of many such visions.

Coonoor, a British Hill Station in the Nilgiri Hills. The hills turn blue with the flowering of the Jacarandas in spring. It is located at the head of the Hulikal ravine approximately 6,000 feet above sea level. It has been described to me as a verdant environment containing a colourful array of wildflowers where cormorants, pipits, thrushes, parakeets and skylarks soar on high and sweep the many watercourses and waterfalls. There is the smell of honeysuckle. The comforts of the altitudinal climate are said to make it a heavenly place for butterflies, bees and babies.

The extensive tea plantations and woodlands invite trekking and hiking for holiday makers who flock to the region to enjoy its natural beauty and attend the numerous festivals held throughout the holiday season. Not far from the centre of the village, on Church Road, near the Shiva Temple, is the bungalow which has been provided for our family. It promises an ideal base for the raising of many children.

The trip is long and arduous. The further we travel the drier the landscape becomes. The horses are sure footed but the road is corrugated and I suffer many hours of misery, sustained by the promise of a pleasant life with many babies. Aunty Banita sits with me and boosts my tolerance with healing herbs and infusions to encourage sleep. I am grateful for the days spent in recovery in Bengaluru within the Cantonment established there in 1809 to house British troops. The streets are orderly and the houses are characterised by the *monkey top* eaves and its lawns and trees, flowers and shrubs are a delight. After this reprieve, the horses and carts continue up the mountains until Coonoor comes within view.

We arrive to helpful hands, tea and traditional British fare. Surprised eyes greet us as I introduce Aunty Banita and Tai to James' colleagues. James had previously warned me of the atmosphere of mistrust which has arisen since the massacres. British wives have taken over the management of households. It seems that a Eurasian wife is an asset, but Indian servants are not. I attempt to defuse this concern by declaring Banita as my Aunt and Tai as my Uncle.

On the first night in our new home James wipes away my tears which have flowed daily since our 'little soldier' passed on. He promises, 'There will be more children, my dear one.' I know this is likely. I have already experienced three miscarriages. Aarchie was our first child to be born naturally having reached maturation.

After a supper of Earl Grey Tea and raisin bun with strawberry jam left by our British neighbours, I retire to bed. The timber shutters gently fan the breeze from the valley below. The clean fresh smell of the surrounding foliage reminds me of wild waterfalls and caves of Yorkshire. One of our first adventures together was when James and I visited Malham Cove, a natural wonder wrought by glaciers that raked the region during the ice ages. The limestone platforms were inspiration for poets, philosophers and painters such as Rusken, Turner and Ward.

James' towering six foot two inch figure cast a shadow over my mere five foot three inch silhouette as we trekked our way to the watercourses. However imposing, his shadow was that of a gentle magnanimous giant. I was not to know that this inherent kindness and tolerance would lead him to such emotional turmoil. His balanced proportions, a handsome face with a fashionable dark moustache, expertly trimmed, were engaging but it was his eyes, the colour of almandine garnet blemished with shots of topaz throughout, which immediately connected with mine. I was enchanted from that moment.

I was twenty two and away from home for the first time having been sent to Britain to complete my education. My college motto was *May they have life and have it more abundantly.*

Papa was acquainted with Alfred, James' father who had served in the British Army in India in the early 1800s. Alfred had married Lucille the daughter of an Indian woman and a French diplomat stationed in Madras. At the end of his service, Alfred returned to York with his wife and young family. James Alfred Brownlee was born in York on 9 May 1822. He followed in the family tradition of Army service. His fair complexion allowed him to be considered good 'British stock'. His French and Indian heritage could be overlooked. It was impossible for me, however, due to my dark skin, brown eyes and my abundant glossy Indian hair to deny my Indian heritage. I wore my hair parted down the middle and drawn into a tight bun at the nape of my neck. James and I had both been raised as Christians but we had the benefit of Indian wisdom imparted to us by our female relations. We were two souls joined by a common heritage.

We saw our future in India. We would help and be helped by India. Was this expecting too much of India or of us?

At the conclusion of his studies in January 1854, James

travelled to India to take up his posting with the British forces in Allahabad. It was the first time he had been to India. I travelled from Pondicherry to join him there. I had previously been to Allahabad with Papa, Rose and Aunty Banita and had climbed the *undying* Banyan Tree, *Akshaivata*, leaping from its boughs in an attempt to achieve salvation from the endless cycle of rebirth and had then travelled to the stupa at Kausambi on the banks of the Yawuna River where it was believed the Buddha had once preached. I planned to take James there so he could also experience its aura of serenity.

James and I were married at the military base in Allahabad. Papa, Rose, *Grand-mére*, Aunty Banita and Tai were in attendance. It was a Christian ceremony conducted in the Chapel followed by refreshments for the wedding party which had been organised by the Commander. Later, James and I slipped away to the sacred *sangam* where the three rivers, the Ganges, Yamuna and the mythical *Saraswati* converge. I told him of the Hindi legend of the *sangam*. The gods and demons were fighting for possession of the *kumbh*, the urn of immortal nectar, *amrit*. Vishnu gave the urn to Garuda, his winged mount. During his flight, four drops of the nectar fell on four places Nask, Ijjain, Haridwar and Allahabad. A k*umbh mela* is held at each of these locations in turn every three years to commemorate this spiritual event.

The planetary configurations were aligned on our wedding night transforming the waters of the Ganges into golden nectar. From a vantage point, James and I declared our love as the golden river of nectar and the hoard of faithful followers, flowed below us in the moonlight.

We rejoined the family the next day. We did not know that this would be the last occasion we would be together.

Fragments of a Life

I sense an impending birth. The source of life, a strong wilful woman longing for motherhood bears down with confident vengeance against past disappointments. A midwife is in attendance. She promises no sadness today. Like a butterfly, breaking through the chrysalis, to enter this new life. Transformed. I squirm as I am raised into the world upside down. A victorious burst of life leaves my body as I cry out in anger at being evicted from the pupa. Applause and laughter fill the arid space like drought-breaking rains as they flood a thirsty landscape. Large gentle hands lift me to safety. They place me on a warm soft body which pulsates with nurture. I am introduced to my mother 'Catherine Rose, this is your mother, Rasna.' Her gentle hands direct my suckling.

Mother. I am not alone, I am safe, I am home.

I will linger within this body to experience the pivotal moments which greet this new generation and their descendants. She is family. I love her as my own. There is hope. There is renewal.

Catherine Rose
Coonor, India

It is 1863. I am five years old today. My Mama and Papa lay sleeping in our home in Coonor in the Nilgiri Hills. I jump between them on the big bed. I snuggle into the space they always make for me. We sleep on. Mama stirs first. She kisses me awake, tickling the vulnerable spot on my neck. I turn clinging to Papa for protection but suffer further gentle tickling at his hands.

I escape them both and run through the house looking for Aunty Banita. I find her in religious reflection in her room. I go and sit beside her. Her grace and calm spread to my body like nectar spreads on hot bread. I mirror her pose. She looks down at me, her grandniece, with loving kindness. I smile and mouth, 'I love you.' She acknowledges the significance. We rise. Her sari brushes across my arm creating the music so comforting to my ears. That sound, so much a part of my life.

I start to dance in circles to the music in my head. I am a ballerina. I am Giselle in Mama's music box. I dance my way into the kitchen. Our dogs, awaiting the hunt later in the day, raise themselves from their post at the door to bark a greeting. Tai is there, as usual, to prevent too much exuberance. The quiet of the early morning returns as the dogs resume their guardianship. The sun rises above the Coonoor woodland below and seeks to make its way through the timber shutters into the kitchen. The smell of wet Jasmine wafts into the room as bees, butterflies and birds alight on its blossom. I watch calm personified as Aunty Banita prepares, as she has always done, food for the family.

Papa and Mama call me to come. I run to their room. They sit supported by large colourful cushions. Papa pats the scarlet bedspread for me to be seated. I look at my mother. Her growing belly is struggling to escape the constraints of her pink satin night gown. I know there is a baby in there but I am tired of waiting for it to arrive.

There, at the centre of the bed, is a parcel beautifully wrapped in colourful paper.

'Happy birthday, Catherine Rose,' they sing. I slowly remove the pink ribbon and its bow and unfold the wrapping. Lying there are pink ballet slippers and a pink tutu.

I smile. I say, 'I will be like *Giselle* in Mama's music box. I will dance for you like *Giselle*.' I look from Papa to Mama. I see that Mama is crying. I go to her and hug her, leaning on her blossoming breasts to kiss her tears away.

'Don't be sad Mama, you will smile when *Giselle* and I dance.'

Catherine Rose

It is 1868. I am ten years old today. I am in my bedroom in our home in Coonoor. It is dark. I can hear my Papa crying. He cries at night, by day he is happy again. My Mama says that he cries for the people who died in the war. Aunty Banita tells me that my Papa is a brave man. He fought in the war when lots of Indian and British people died. He remembers their faces, their pain. She says I must always love my Papa and show him I love him every day.

Yesterday a soldier arrived with a large leather bag. He handed it to Papa. He called Mama.

'It's my father's bag,' she said when she saw it, 'the one Tai said was made of dead pigs.'

She stroked the dark shiny leather and pressed her fingers into the embossed gold name *Dr Aziz*, then felt along its edges, worn bare like scuffed shoes from too much walking. She opened the fold-down sides and leaning over retrieved a bound volume.

'It's father's diary,' she said. She placed it on the dining table, opening it at the bookmark protruding from the gilt-edged pages.

She read:

"*Cawnpore.*

July 23rd, 1857: Rose, Maman and I have survived a night under siege at the hands of the natives. There are several families here with us. We found shelter in the cellar below the barracks. Those who refused to join us were slaughtered during the night as they lay sleeping. The sound of children screaming as they were wrenched from their mother's arms, will always remain with me, as will the cries of the mothers as their children were beheaded in front of them. The killing continued during a night of torture. Helpless, we covered our ears to prevent the horror sending us mad. The smell of death however invaded our senses. In the morning, through a ventilation grill in the cellar wall, I witnessed the natives, drunk with power, proceed to cart the bodies to the well and in a final act of barbarism local butchers hacked them into disposable pieces throwing them into the well. When the rampaging ceased the natives and the butchers ran off and all was quiet.

July 24th 1857. Venturing into the quadrangle, we found several slain soldiers lying there. I rushed to one young man who was still alive. Two of our company carried him into the cellar. Rose and Maman and I tended him, cleaning his wounds, applying bandages and dripping water into his swollen mouth. He was unable to speak coherently. He kept on calling for his mother. Rose and Maman sat with him all day. Maman told him, 'It is your mother here my son and I will look after you now.' He died in her arms several hours later. When darkness hid the horror the men returned to the barracks with flickering candles and found correspondence ordering the Commander to stand fast as there was a rescue force on its way from Allahabad. Small quantities of food and drink were salvaged and brought into the cellar.

July 25th 1857. When the food ran out it was decided that the only chance of survival was to make our way to the river, find a boat and make it to the fort downstream. When it was dark, our company travelled the short distance to the river. A boat hidden in the reeds was discovered and with the sound of gunfire and the sight of flames in the distance, we boarded the boat, covered ourselves with matting and allowed the river to take us where it flowed.

July 26th 1857. This morning at dawn the fort appeared through the mist. British soldiers stood guard. They helped us ashore. The Commander has negotiated a safe passage for us to continue our journey down the river. This will be my last entry. I will leave this diary with the Commander. God willing we will make our way safely back to Pondicherry."

Mama closes the diary. Papa embraces her. He knows the fate of those brave souls. They were fired upon and their funeral pyre carried them into heaven. Papa was part of the rescue force which arrived too late to save them.

Catherine Rose
Off the coast of Launceston. Tasmania

It is 1876. I am 18 years old. The Brownlee family which comprises Mama Rasna, Papa James myself and my brothers, twins James Alfred and Edgar Charles, Archie Alexander and my twin sisters Lucille Rasna and Elizabeth Rosalie gather together on the deck of *The Tamar* which is transporting us to Launceston. Our new homeland comes into view across the steel-grey waters of Bass Strait.

Before departing India, my dear Aunty Banita passed

away and shortly thereafter, old Tai also. Aunty Banita was given a Christian burial in accordance with her wish not to be burnt. She lies with my brother Aarchie in the Pondicherry cemetery.

Papa has secured a grant of land for his good works in India. The Tasmanian Government offered those of 'British stock' the opportunity to help build a new country. My brothers and Papa are excited. They will be farmers in a cool, wet land which they have been told is like England.

Whilst my family is full of hope for the future, I wipe tears from my eyes. I have had to leave behind my dear husband of three years and our two babies. They were taken by cholera's cruelty. To add to this cruelty is the sorrow I feel at having been left to go on without them in a foreign land. My only solace is the knowledge that they are being cared for by our dearly departed in heaven and that one day, we will be reunited.

Papa says women have to rage against what life unfairly hands them. He says it is like fighting an unfair war. He speaks from experience. He says we are both warriors. We must be brave. Our hope is that peace is ahead of us in this new land.

Mama says the secret to a better life for women and men is education. She has continued my education during the long voyage. I have been reading books and newspaper articles on Tasmania which have been provided to us on board the Steamer.

Catherine Rose
Mount Dismal. Tasmania

It is 1877. I am 19 years old. Our new home is about 20 miles from Launceston. The atmosphere is *other worldly*. My dark skin, Indian hair and eyes set me apart from our neighbours. In India, my family was treated with respect and regard notwithstanding the Indian push for independence. In my new home there is no deference afforded. On the contrary, there is a scowl of indifference. There is something else, an underlying distrust, one might even observe, fear. The words 'black' 'half caste' 'native' pass their lips as they walk by. Papa is the first to recognise this change in our status. He describes it as mistrust and disgust.

Mama is more concerned with the daily struggle to survive in this harsh land – putting food on the table and clothes on our backs. The clothes we brought with us seem comically inappropriate here. The crinoline, satin and lace gowns and the silk saris inherited from Aunty Banita lay silently awaiting further instructions in the big metal trunk pushed into a corner of Mama's room. It is summer and we girls are all clothed in loose fitting cotton dresses which resemble nightgowns. Mama wears cotton saris in the house.

I seek out the local newspapers which Mama and I read as we prepare the evening meal. My teenage brothers have forsaken their education for outdoor activities and the pursuit of liquor and girls. They work as timber men, cutting and gathering trees or in the tin or slate mines. Papa's dream for them to be farmers in a cool climate has not yet materialised. The land granted to him for his good works in India for the British is many miles away from the nearest settlement. It is heavily wooded. Papa says you can't even grow a potato because of the heavy frosts during the growing season. Consequently, the boys' value is in their labour. I watch them as they venture into the forest of massive trees each day. They return with stories of snakes, lizards, devils and the wallabies they have encountered. The trees stand at the edge of the area cleared for our home, like soldiers on guard. They create an impenetrable line protecting their land against invaders.

I focus on what is different, not what is the same in this new land. The smell is different. There is no background smell of India. Whilst our home smells like India with curries and rice still a staple diet in our home, in the community, the smell is of eucalyptus burning. The people are different. They are white. The only black person I see is a young Aboriginal girl who spies on me from behind trees as I walk the back road to the settlement. I have seen her family. They live apart, separated from the white populace. Her black eyes always connect with mine. They ask, 'are you like me?' I look away. Something inside me wants to say 'yes' but then I see how she and her family are treated so I deny this and become like all those around me, I deny her the connection to humanity. I do not tell Mama I do this.

Our homestead was constructed of split timber palings. The massive trees were sawn through with a huge crosscut saw which sang and moaned its way through the tree culminating with the boss calling 'timber'. As the mighty soldiers fell upon the ground, the smell of the natural world escaped into the air like the smell of blood flowing from a knife's cut into flesh. The felled trees were dragged by horses to the timber mill and cut into manageable palings. Our neighbour, Mr Watson provided the horse team and the dray in return for my brothers' labour.

My sisters and I provide cleaning, stitching and cooking for the community.

Another difference is the number of people. This land is empty. You can travel the roads and not see anyone for days then from the forest you can hear them, rough loud voices threatening their horses and their dogs if they fail to heed their commands. The chains on the drays rattle across timber planked bridges. Obscenities ring out through the forest. The words have become familiar to my brothers much to Mama's disgust.

In the afternoon after our work is done and it is still light, we young ones grab bread from the pantry, wrap it in a kerchief and head down to the waterfall a mile away. I love it there. I feel heaven must be like this place. It is cool and the tree ferns wave at me as I pass. Lizards scuttle out of the way. My favourite rock stands smooth and warm ready to slide me into the cool running water. Birds of many colours start squabbling about their preferred positions before nestling down for the night. Early to bed they raise us from our slumbers at dawn with their calls to action.

A common joy is growing within the local community. Names and faces are becoming known and accepted. The children play happily together. We no longer have to explain where we come from, why we have different coloured skin and why our mother resembles an *Indian squaw* and that we are from India not America.

The best time of the day is when the ice man arrives and drops three big blocks of ice on our verandah. They are quickly covered with hessian bags to slow the melting. The young ones rush to sit on the blocks and chip away at the edges. Mama whips them away like they were the huge flies which invade every part of our lives. The big blue flies even try to escape the heat by invading our mouths. Mama sits on the verandah in the rocking chair crafted by my brothers. She is plump again. The birth is expected near Christmas. The last birth in India, the twelfth child, a boy, William Joseph did not survive. He remains with the others of our family dearly departed being cared for by Aunty Banita and Tai until we are all re-united in heaven.

My Papa has procured a position for me as a nanny with the Police Constable's family. It is my first day. On my way to their home I see the black girl who spies on me from behind the towering trees. Today she stands in front of this tall white tree the locals call a ghost gum. Three black cockatoos are perched above her head like sentinels. Her hair is matted but her skin is glossy as though she has been dipped in black oil. Her teeth, like white tombstones greet me with a smile as I stop. Today I am ready to say hello.

As I turn towards her she disappears into the tree leaving a red stain on the white bark. The black cockatoos swoop down towards me then turn, flashing their yellow tail feathers at me. Their cry is one of pain as they fly off in single formation towards the sun. I stand for several minutes as if in a trance. I go to the ghost gum and run my hand along the gash which oozes red sticky gum. I rub the gum on the bark to clean my fingers. I return to the path. Confused, I say out loud, 'I will have to ask Mama to explain this to me,' before continuing along the path.

My first day as a nanny is a delight. The children are Caroline aged eighteen months and Frederick aged four. Caroline stretches out her arms towards me. Frederick shows me his coloured wooden soldier, asking me to play with him. Their mother, Emily, a well-spoken lady with red flowing hair and an engaging smile welcomes me into her home. She seems to know about my loss. She asks me to treat her children as my own. I help her feed them and I put them to bed. My heart is crying for my own babies. I do what Papa has told me to do, I say to my babies in heaven, 'Mama will love you through these children. When I cradle them asleep I am cradling you. When I laugh with them I am playing with you.'

When they are asleep I sit with Emily and have tea and scones. After tea I help her clean out some old newspapers. They are The Mercury which Mama reads with me. I ask if I can take some of these newspapers home. She is happy for this to occur and hands me one of the newspapers which speaks of the last Black Tasmanian, a woman named Truganini, who has just died. I am prompted to tell her of my experience with the black girl and the ghost gum. She says, 'you must be mistaken. There are no black people left in Tasmania now, except for you, of course, but you are not an Aboriginal, you are Indian.' I leave her home confused but happy.

On the way past the ghost gum I wave The Mercury paper at the tree and say, 'Good night, Truganini. I will see you tomorrow.'

When I reach home, I tell Mama and Papa about my first day as a nanny. I tell Papa I did as he told me and I wasn't sad, but I do not tell them about the black girl and the ghost gum. I go to bed after saying my prayers to God and Aunty Banita asking them to protect me and my loved ones. As I close my eyes I enter that other world:

You know she is a vision from the past but for you she is in the present. She smiles at you. The white tombstone teeth speak of death but the smile is so sweet that the spectre holds no fear. There is no terror. You lift the kerosene lamp high like a beacon to lead her to you and into the golden nectar glow which surrounds you. You stand to attention, alert and ready to respond to her approach. She is a timid creature of the forest, you must treat her as such. No sudden movements, keep your eyes focused on her, engage her soul, her inner being, draw her in, welcoming her into the present.

I awake refreshed and ready for the day. The dawn sky discloses a forest bereft of all nocturnal life. The scream of the devils no longer rings out. Their eyes no longer pierce the darkness with their evil glow. There is no black girl, no spirit of a forgotten people. I look down at my upturned hand. I turn it over. My black hand now displays a pattern of white dots.

Truganini's stories come to me through my visions. I call on her whenever I pass the ghost gum. I focus on the white dots on my dark hand which only I can see. Her experiences mirror those of my female ancestors in another land, India. Rape, incest, violence, hatred, murder are all part of the female experience at the hands of the powerful. The female of the species is vulnerable and disposable.

Emily, my employer's wife, is different. She has taken it upon herself to assume a position of power. She introduces me to the members of the local Church and I become a member of the Temperance movement. The group promotes the moderation rather than the abstinence of alcohol. It provides alternative venues for the men to meet after their work is done. Coffee palaces have replaced some of the hotels. Papa and Mama encourage my brothers to frequent these alternatives with little success so far.

On my way home, as I pass Truganini's tree. I see her face, etched in the whiteness of the ghost gum. She does not smile. I cannot see those white tombstone teeth. Tears of blood ebb and flow from her soul, turning her cheeks from black to red. I approach with outstretched arms ready to comfort and console. Her sentinels, the black cockatoos, sweep down upon me preventing me from any contact.

I return home. I retire to my bed without supper. As I close my eyes, I enter that other world:

You know what you see is a vision from the past but to you it is the present. You see Truganini's people running through the long grass. Behind them are many white men with rifles which they discharge into the air. Some of these men are in uniform whilst others are in civilian dress. Some hold farming implements instead of rifles. It is the 7th day of October 1830 and Truganini's people are running for their lives. They are being herded like wild animals. The smoke from the fires lit by the pursuers reaches their eyes and noses. The soldiers are following orders to capture, but the volunteers, the farmers and free settlers, seek revenge for the deaths of their family and friends at the hands of the natives. Others, the ticket of leave convicts seek favour for their efforts having been promised a bounty for each skull claimed. Many are primed with alcohol which has been provided to them from the numerous public houses along the way. A band of womenfolk follow their men with food and clothes.

Within days, the weather becomes unfavourable. The wind

howls and the snow begins to fall and the men, ill prepared for these conditions, crawl on hands and knees over craggy rocks. They are forced to stop their advancement and make camp. The gaps created in the Black Line makes escape easy for those being herded. Soon Truganini's people are safely back in familiar territory whilst the civilian force is losing its initial enthusiasm to kill the black bastards and is focused on survival.

The settlers' homes, now only maintained by their women and children become the native's prey. The volunteers, their feet and backs worn thin like masticated chewing tobacco, abandon the Black Line and return to their homes. The 'official' aim, to capture hostile natives and drive them to the Tasmanian Peninsula where they will be secured in that place, has failed. The 'official' record counts two natives captured and two natives killed.

Truganini's people are representative of all the Indigenous groups in Tasmania. They know they are fighting for survival now, having accepted they are on the brink of collapse. In the past, their women suffered rape at the hands of the white male populace, due in part to the lack of women to service their sexual appetites, but due also to the violent nature of the transported men who have nothing more to lose in this brutal place. The destruction of their environment and their source of food has made them susceptible to introduced diseases. Many have died from these diseases. The native women have born children to the rapists. They have been prevented or have chosen not to return to their native homes. Their menfolk have conducted revenge killings and have attacked the settlers in their attempts to recover their women. Many on both sides have died.

Following the Black Line campaign, in the face of extermination, the natives attack homesteads for food. The primary motivation now is survival.

I awake, full of the sorrow etched on Truganini's face.

As I walk the path to my employment that day, the trees are wailing their sadness as witnesses to the horror visited upon the forest and the natives. The wind tells of the rape, murder and disease. I begin to understand how the destruction of a race resulted from the destruction of their environment. Areas of forest were laid bare in fits of angry pride and retaliation against the forces of nature which had hindered their progress during the failed campaign. As a result of the destruction of their environment it was inevitable that the pure black lineage of Tasmania would be wiped out.

I am unable to find any joy in my contact with the children in my care today. When the children and their mother retire to their beds to avoid the oppressive heat of the afternoon and the house is quiet I stretch out on a mat on the verandah. A gentle cool breeze like my dear husband's breath on my body causes me to unbutton my blouse and unwind my hair letting it flow freely. I fall into a deep sleep. I stir. I cannot breathe. There is a python like constriction to my torso. My eyes fight their way into consciousness. I try to focus. A face is pushed against mine. The body lies on mine. Alcoholic breath fills my mouth. All I see is one big bloodshot eye which rises and falls as his body part enters me over and over again. I try to cry out but I am struck dumb with fear and pain. At last, the scream of a black cockatoo escapes from my throat. He stops. He lifts his body off mine sufficient to punch me in the face. I enter that other world:

I look down at my body. I see a boy I recognise doing unspeakable things to me. I do not feel the pain. My cotton skirt is up around my neck. My legs are splayed like a dead animal ready for carving. The boy stands above me now, buttoning his fly. He staggers from the verandah. I see the children standing at the doorway. They run inside calling for their mother. Emily comes. She covers my nakedness but she cannot cover my shame. She places my head gently on a pillow and applies a cold compress to my smashed face. She is crying angry tears. She tells Frederick to fetch papa and the doctor.

I re-enter my body. I am met by unspeakable pain from my shattered nose. Emily welcomes me back - 'You will be alright my dear you are safe.' I open my mind to the possibility of survival. I will be brave. I will find a way to escape this evil as the natives did in this cruel land.

Fragments of a Life

New lives in a new land.. They are evolutionary, mutants, hybrids for a new generation. Born on the same day, they will share the same world but they come with different parentage. Souls conjoined by circumstances of birth. The source of the nectar is irrelevant. Whether from butterfly or bee it is still nectar. It is capable of nurturing and sustaining life. The nectar they provide is sweet and satisfying and is shared.

Rosemary
George Town. Northern Tasmania

It is 1878. My name is Rosemary. I have been held here at the old Female Factory in George Town since I got too sick to survive on the streets of Launceston. My 'crime' was getting pregnant. I have now given birth to my daughter, Rosanna. She has been taken away from me because I cannot look after her. I am dying. No, it is not the result of childbirth but my unfortunate lifestyle. I am another in a long line of females forced into prostitution to survive in this godless land. My great grandmother was a convict who arrived in Van Diemen's Land on *The Harmony* in 1829 and was held in the Female Factory in Hobart Town. She had no name in that terrible place. She was known as Number 53.

I know my family history because the people in this place

knew her and her daughter Mary Rose and her granddaughter Mary Anne.

Mary Rose was just a number when she was reclaimed, like an umbrella from a cloak room, at the age of five. The story goes that her mother, No 53, came to the orphanage dressed in black lace. She wore a scarlet hat on top of her curly auburn hair. Her lips were smudged red and she smelt of liquor. The orphanage, glad to reduce their numbers, was happy to release the child to her care. At last she had kept her promise to the child. She hugged her daughter to her breasts all the way to her home, a boarding house of ill repute in Hobart Town.

Mary Rose described her mother as kind and loving when she was not drinking but, when drunk, she was cruel and incapable of caring for her. What followed was ten years of confusion, violence, separation, foster-homes and ultimately, at the age of fifteen, Mary Rose stood at the graveside of her dead mother. Her name, Sarah, not her number 53, appeared on the headstone, paid for by her common law husband. He was last seen entering the Gloucester Arms Hotel for 'another pint or two to see the old girl off.'

After her mother's death, Mary Rose was able to locate her twin brother, Daniel, who had been released from an orphanage in Launceston. They continued to lead a life not unlike their mother's. Theft and prostitution came easily. Mary Rose spent many years in the George Town Female Factory for drunkenness and aggressive behaviour.

Eventually, whilst assigned as a domestic, she took up with an escaped convict. Together they survived by stealing from the wealthy.

When they had enough money, they bought land, gave up the grog and turned respectable, settling down to raise a family. Their children, including my mother, Mary Anne, blossomed. Sadly, the joy ended when they were recognised as escapees. They were apprehended and jailed. At the age of ten, my mother Mary Anne, ran away from her foster home and joined a gang of larrikins roaming around Launceston. She survived by stealing and selling her body. It wasn't long before she contracted a venereal disease. At age thirteen, she gave birth to twins, like her female forebears. We were born in the walls of the Female Factory.

I spent my youth in an orphanage where I was given a basic education. I can read and write. When I was fourteen I went to live with Daniel and his gang of *larrikins* on the streets of Launceston. They became my family. It was there that I became pregnant with my girl Rosanna. I now await death. My dear little Rosanna is safe. She has gone to live with her grandparents, Rasna and James. Her father, Archie Alexander left Tasmania and works somewhere on the mainland. I pray every day that Rosanna will not follow her female forebears into prostitution and crime. It only leads to misery and abuse and a short life. 'Dear God please have mercy on my child.'

You know you are entering another world. As you lie there, awaiting death, you see a lyrebird sitting at the end of the bed. Its tail is fanned in a courtship display. This bird is a flawless mimicker who has the ability to remember the forest sounds of over 200 years. The older bird passes onto its young the sounds it learned from its parents. The sacred lineal knowledge is transported to the next generation. The instinctive sounds are heard by the young as if through their ancestors' ears.

The bird speaks: 'You have carried with you into this life all that your ancestors have experienced and encountered and understood. Without explanation, justification or rationale, you have accepted that knowledge. I will visit with your descendants and help them to understand your life choices and put them into context and help them to make different choices.'

A smile of peaceful repose transforms her face in death.

Fragments of a Life

Spawned from sorrow and hate? No matter. The butterfly's descendants hold all the hope of the future within the chrysalis. I enter the lives of this new generation. Will they be able to break free from the unfortunate lives of their ancestors? What has remained from the past and what new experiences will they send forward. Can they change the world?

Rosanna

Mount Dismal. Tasmania

It is 1883. My name is Rosanna. I am five years old. I live with my grandmother Rasna and my grandfather James in Tasmania. My mother, Rosemary, was unable to keep me with her when I was born. I think she was sent away by her parents after my birth. I think she was sick. I have never met my mother or her family. My father Archie Alexander travelled to the mainland looking for work after my birth. I will find him one day and tell him I love him. He writes to me and sends me pictures of birds, butterflies and flowers. He is a gardener in a large house in a place called Melbourne. For my birthday he sent me a card with a picture of a lyrebird on it. He wrote that these birds inhabit the gardens in Melbourne.

My Aunty, Catherine Rose, is my adopted mother. Both she and I look like Grandma Rasna. We look Indian, but Aunty says, 'we are Tasmanian.'

Veeda is Aunty's daughter. Aunty calls us her twins because we were born on the same day. Veeda has fair skin like Grandpa James. We three, Veeda, Aunty and I sleep together in a big bed in the room my Uncles built when we were born. There is a big window which looks out on the forest. Every morning when we wake we say hello to the forest. The trees wave back. We laugh a lot and cuddle one another on those cold frosty mornings. Grandpa James comes in and tries to tickle us so that we have to get out of bed. He is getting old and stiff and cannot chase us very far so we always win the race back to bed. He then goes to stoke the fire in the parlour ready for Aunty to sit while she tends to her knitting. She does not go out very often in public. She does not have a husband. A very bad man hurt her. She wears a silk veil to cover her face. It was Grandma Rasna's veil when she was a young girl. It is beautiful. It has butterflies on it. Aunty wears it when she tends to her bee hives which are in the forest behind the house. She is known around town as the 'butterfly lady'.

The Police Constable's wife, Emily, comes to visit her every Saturday and brings her cake and we spend time with her children, Caroline and Frederick. Aunty gives her jars of honey to take home. We have honey every day on hot bread straight from the oven. We also, as a special treat, get the honeycomb sometimes. In the summer, after school is out, Aunty, Veeda and I walk to the nearby waterfall. On the way we visit Truganini. Aunty places flowers at the foot of the white gum and talks to her.

Because Veeda's skin and hair are fair and my skin and hair are dark Grandpa James says, 'you girls are different sides of the same coin.' Veeda and I laugh when he says this and we sing out 'give us the coin Grandpa.' He chases us, and when he catches us, we get tickled.

We have three uncles who go away to work in the mines. We don't see them very often but when they visit they go to the public houses, come home drunk and fight a lot.

I saw one of them pick up a flat iron from the stove and throw it. It just missed Grandma on the other side of the room. Grandpa got the shovel and chased the boys out the front door. 'Don't come back until you are sober.'

Uncle Willie, William Henry, is the youngest brother, not much older than Veeda and I. He is a Tasmanian he tells us 'born and bred'. Willie says he isn't going to grow up to be a drinker. 'I'm going to get an education, get married and go to the mainland to work,' he says.

Sadness filled the valley today. There is a memorial service to be held for Aunty Catherine's twin sisters Lucille Rasna and Elizabeth Rosalie who were drowned when the boat they were travelling in to visit my father Archie Alexander in Melbourne capsized in a violent storm on Bass Strait. The Church is packed with locals who weep along with our family. Their bodies were never recovered. Aunty Catherine sits in the front row next to Grandma Rasna and Grandpa James. Her face is covered by her butterfly veil. She holds a tapestry created by both Lucille and Elizabeth. My grandmother Rasna and grandfather James present the tapestry to Reverend Dowling for display in the Church. Reverend Dowling accepts the gift and confirms a plaque will be placed below the tapestry in memory of the twins. After the service we travel to the waterfall where the family sit on the smooth rocks and recall the times the twins laughed and sang and played in the cool water after their work was done. Aunty Catherine also recalls how they would sit on the ice when it was delivered to the house and Grandma Rasna would swat them away with her apron as they picked at the ice. The twins never married. They were dedicated to helping my grandparents and the community. They were so close they completed one another's sentences. They were proud of Willie and were on their way to Melbourne to try and encourage Archie Alexander to return to Tasmania to be near to me his daughter.

The smell of the eucalyptus and honeysuckle go with us as we return home. Grateful for having had Lucille and Elizabeth in our lives. When we arrive home twins James and Edgar are there with the dinner cooking on the stove. It is the girls favourite curry. We go to our beds full of curry and apple pie and Willie's squeeze box filling our ears with his music. I still pray that my father will come back to be with me.

It is 1888. I am ten years old. Aunty warns me of the *larrikins* who roam town looking for trouble. Some people call them *Arabs* because they have no permanent home. They are nomads, living by their wits trying to survive in a cruel world not of their making. Their behaviour is generally excused by the authorities, but when they become violent and injure people they are labelled *ruffians* and if captured by the authorities, they are sent away for retraining.

The boy who hurt Aunty roamed with a band of *larrikins*

in Launceston. His name was Daniel. My father Archie ran away from home and roamed Launceston with Daniel's gang until Grandpa caught up with him, gave him a whipping with his belt and a good talking to and dragged him home to sober up and get back to work.

Ruffians like Daniel terrorised the local community. They stole alcohol and went on drunken rampages damaging property, attacking and injuring people and raping the local girls.

Daniel was apprehended and charged with rape. He was placed in a reformatory for a short time and then transferred to one of the Government's industrial training facilities. This lenient treatment was the policy of the Courts who considered these boys to be 'victims' who needed help, not punishment. Aunty agrees that as a child of homeless parents who were the descendants of convicts, Daniel should be given the opportunity to show he can be a worthwhile member of the community. However, there are no jobs and, like the urchins in the large British cities, they, through necessity, turn to crime to survive. Girls from these families turn to prostitution. They are usually young, even as young as ten years old. If they get sick they are housed in the female factories which have been transformed into places for the sick, homeless, and troubled where they can be cared for.

I ask Aunty, 'Was my mother Rosemary one of these girls?' Aunty says, 'Yes, she was, but we should be kind to her memory because she died from a disease she caught while trying to support herself without a proper family.' Grandma says, 'Concentrate on your school work young lady and you'll grow up to be a fine woman.' That's easy, I enjoy going to school. I like learning.

It is 1893. I am fifteen years old. Aunty Catherine runs a stall at the local market where she sells her honey. Veeda and I help her. The golden nectar glows from its jars on the shelves in the stall. I am *'the artistic one'*, according to Grandma, so I designed a label and a billboard which shows Aunty wearing her butterfly scarf and holding a jar of her honey. I also like gardening. I have been growing lavender. The boys helped me dig up an area near the house. They brought mulch from the floor of the forest and mixed it with chook poo.

I have learnt the art of soap making. I have created lavender scented soap which is sold at the market stall. Veeda uses the distilled oil from the lavender to produce a medicinal preparation for stomach complaints, to calm the nerves and ease itchy skin. She also burns the oil to help Aunty's breathing through her damaged nose.

Veeda is beautiful. Her hair and skin are fair. Grandma Rasna says she resembles her sister Rose who died many years ago. Veeda is very smart. She has received merit certificates for excellence in Attendance, English and Social Studies. She wants to be a doctor when she grows up so she can help people, especially help to repair Aunty's shattered nose and rebuild her face so she will no longer have to hide her face.

Veeda has been reading about the Suffragettes. She has been telling me about Catherine Helen Spence who lives in South Australia. She is campaigning for women's right to vote. Her hero is Vida Goldstein who is the President of the Federal Women's Political Association on the mainland. Veeda says she is described in the newspaper as 'a dangerous and persuasive woman'. I think Veeda wants to be a dangerous and persuasive woman too.

My Uncle Willie has a cow in calf now. Mr Watson, our neighbour, gave it to him as payment for his assistance with his herd while he was recovering from a stroke. Willie likes cows. He wants to get a herd of dairy cows. He will be able to provide the family and the community with milk.

Willie is strong. He can lift things normally requiring two men. Because of his dark skin he is often taken for an Aboriginal. He treats the jibes in a humorous way.

'Unfortunately I'm not a native. I'm just an Indian wrestler here on holidays.' This is followed by a flexing of his muscles.

He is popular with the girls. When he walks down the road the girls rush to their front gates inviting him in for lemonade.

On Sunday Willie and I went to watch Walter Challis, the champion axeman, Willie's hero, compete.

When we arrived, Willie bought me lemonade and peanuts and we sat in the stand. All at once, Willie jumped to his feet.

'I'll be back later to take you home.'

I watched as he headed towards this girl standing near the lemonade stand. She had blonde hair and a happy face. Willie lifted himself to his full height as he talked to her then rolled up his shirt sleeves showing off his muscles. He bought her lemonade and some lollies. They sat together in the seats below me.

Challis won the competition. I saw Willie kissing the girl goodbye.

He came back to take me home. 'Who is the girl, Willie,?' I asked.

'That's my girl, Maudie,' he said. 'She doesn't know it yet but I'm going to marry her.' I giggled. 'Don't laugh,' says Willie, 'You just wait, when I have my own place I'll ask her to marry me.'

It wasn't long before Maudie was a frequent visitor to our home.

Before these visits, Willie makes us help him tidy the house. He picks large bunches of roses to decorate the parlour and puts lavender soap beside the wash basin and water jug. Veeda and I sing, 'Willie's got a girl' over and over again. When he eventually loses patience with us, he chases us down the paddock. We fall into the long yellow grass, happy and satisfied like having just finished one of Aunty's roast chicken dinners.

Maudie is nice. She is like Veeda and I. She giggles a lot. She is shy and doesn't say much but she hangs on every word

Willie says, even silly things that we know he makes up to impress her. On her visit today he told her he could lift her up if she stood on the end of the shovel. She did not dare him to do this feat so Veeda and I did.

'Show us, Willie, show us how strong you are.'

'No, it's ok, I believe you, Willie,' says Maudie but Willie accepts our challenge. We all go outside. He grabs a spade and Maudie stands on the flat metal. He raises her off the ground. Maudie screeches like a white cockatoo and jumps off.

Veeda and I applaud. 'Ok, Willie, you are strong'.

After supper, Willie and Maudie take off down the hill towards the waterfall where lovers go in the evenings.

Willie and Maudie got married today. It is one year since I first saw Maudie and Willie kissing at the wood chopping competition. Our family attended the wedding at the local church. Maudie's brother, Paul, gave her away. Her sister, Flora, also attended. Her mother and father have passed on. She looked pretty in her mother's lace wedding dress. Willie made her a bouquet of pink roses, angel's breath and maiden hair fern for her to hold as the preacher declared them husband and wife. We all dressed up for the occasion. The dresses in Grandma Rasna's trunk came out and were refashioned. Many photographs were taken.

A party was held at our home. It was a warm moonlit night. The stars twinkled above the guests and Willie and

Maudie danced as the fiddler played. When it was time for them to leave, they rode off in the sulky with Willie's champion horse, Geronimo, leading the way down the hill towards their new home. Grandma and Grandpa went to bed early leaving the young ones to party on.

The next day the house groaned and moaned in the heat as if it was suffering a hangover. With help Grandma and Grandpa, in silence, cleaned up the remains of what all declared was a good night.

It is six months since their wedding. The family is going to visit Willie and Maudie today. Their house is on Grandma and Grandpa's land but it is over the ridge so we cannot see it from our house. Willie, with the help of his friends and our Uncles built the house using Tasmanian Oak. As we pass over the hill the house comes into view. The fences and corrals are in place. Willie's dairy cows and his horses graze on the meadow grass. There are also temporary sheds for milking.

When we arrive, Maudie comes to the door. She is wearing a smock which shows off her baby bump. Veeda and I giggle and call Willie '*papa*' all afternoon. He just smiles and looks at Maudie with admiration.

The house is full of flowers contained in old milk pails. Maudie opens our housewarming gifts, a pottery vase created by Aunty Catherine. I have added ceramic lavender sprays and pink roses to its sides. Veeda has sewn lavender into a small pillow which has butterflies embroidered on it. Maudie puts some water in the vase and transfers some of the roses from the pails into it and places it on the dining table.

She holds the lavender pillow to her tummy. A knowing smile beams her thanks.

Willie takes us on a tour of the house. There are only two rooms so it doesn't take long. The front room is the living area with easy chairs and a dining table. The back room is the bedroom. The nursery is in the corner. A cradle stands ready for their first child. A rocking chair is placed next to it. A colourful patchwork quilt is draped over the back of the chair and netting hangs from the ceiling over the cradle, to protect the newborn. The kitchen is outback with a fuel stove and washing facilities. A steel metal bath sits in the centre of the room, ready for hot water from the stove.

Grandpa pats Willie on the shoulder then shakes his hand long and hard.

'I'm proud of you, my son,' he says, 'You are a fine man.'

We sit outside under the big gum. It is hot. Maudie brings us lemonade and sugar biscuits. Grandma and Grandpa and Aunty have billy tea with milk from Willie's cows.

As I lie looking up at the sun through the leaves of the gum I go to another place. I have a dream. I see two little girls, one black and one white both in pink tutus and ballet slippers. They dance to the music of *Giselle*. There is a man sitting in a red chair applauding them. An Indian lady watches them from the door. When I wake I tell Aunty Catherine of my dream.

She smiles. 'You have inherited the gift,' she says.

'What is the gift?' I ask.

'You will see things which will help you live a good life in the service of others. These visions are from those who came before you.'

Fragments of a Life

Beginnings and endings. They are part of nature. Happy welcomings and sad farewells. A life well lived is the ultimate goal. The butterfly lives for a short time but achieves much. Each butterfly's duty is to provide protection, nurture and succour for future generations through the pupa. The humble bee, on the other hand, has evolved with the remarkable habit of social altruism. It is prepared to die to ensure the survival of the hive. The common good prevails. Will we be born a butterfly or a bee? Is this governed by hypothetical sneezes and converging pathways, the contingent frailty of the event chain that leads to our existence? At the end of a life when one counts up achievements and failures are these predictable having regard to those who spawned us, endowing us with measurable qualities, or is it pure chance? The gene governs the physical whilst the meme governs the cultural. They both join in making us who we become. I travel towards a new generation, in a new place.

Beryl

South Sydney. New South Wales

It is 1921. I am Beryl. I am five years old today. I would like a doll of my own for my birthday. I would like one that has yellow hair and blue eyes. My mother, Maudie, chose my name. She says Beryl is a gemstone. Pure beryl is colourless, but if it is flawed, tinted by impurities, it can be yellow or green.

My father, Willie, had given my mother a piece of beryl from the local slate mine near where they lived in a place called Tasmania. It's colour is yellow, like golden honey. She keeps it in the small cedar jewellery box on her dresser in the bedroom. I am not allowed to touch it.

I have a brother Kenneth and a sister Vivian. They are older than me. They were born in Tasmania. I was born in Sydney. My father Willie got sick and had to leave the dairy farm. He decided to move the family to the mainland. My mother tells me she lost twin babies one black one white at birth just before they left for the mainland.

I am fair skinned like my mother. My Mama says my eyes are hazel, a mixture of colours some brown, some green, some blue, but when I look in the mirror they look green.

My brother and sister have dark skin like our father, Willie. Their eyes are brown. My mother says I am like her family who were British. She says her grandfather was a surgeon to Queen Victoria.

Papa always takes Vivian with him and leaves me at home with my Mama. Mama says he is protecting Vivian because cruel people call her nigger when she goes out. One day she came home from school in tears because a boy called out 'nigger, nigger pull the trigger.'

I was outside the house with Papa one day when a neighbour came by. He remarked to my Papa that I was a pretty little girl.

My Papa said, 'Yes, but you should see my other daughter, Vivian, she is beautiful.' I went back in the house and hugged Mama. It hurt my feelings when he said that.

Mama said, 'Why are you crying?'

I couldn't tell her. She kissed me and told me to go and get an icy block from the shop.

It is 1926. I am ten years old. Today we are cleaning and tidying the house ready for a visit from Papa's sister Catherine Rose. She has had an operation and she wants to show Papa her new face. Her daughter Veeda is coming with her. Veeda is a nurse in a big hospital in Melbourne. She helps with operations. She married a doctor she met at the hospital.

Mama looks upset as she checks the house before the visitors arrive. All that she can afford is white butcher paper on the big kitchen table. The lovely tablecloths she had embroidered for her glory box have long gone. The takings from the shop are less these days. The depression has started to affect the country. People are losing their jobs. They have less to spend. My Mama goes to the local fish shop at 5 o'clock each morning to scrub the floors for fish and some extra money. This helps us survive, but it's not enough to buy a new tablecloth.

When Catherine Rose and Veeda arrive, Papa shows off by jumping the fence to greet them. Mama looks away in horror knowing the pain he will suffer later. We all sit around the big kitchen table. I sit in the corner where I have scribbled on the butcher paper much to Mama's annoyance. I cover it with my hands as much as I can. Mama has made scones with cream and strawberry jam and a large teapot full of strong black tea. There is a jug of cold milk. The cups and plates are not ours. They have been borrowed. Old Mrs Harris next door has lent them to Mama for the day. Papa keeps on looking at his sister. He has tears in his eyes. 'You are beautiful, Catherine Rose', he says. 'Thank you, Willie,' she giggles. She becomes that young girl he knew in his youth. 'I always felt beautiful,' she says, 'Now I look beautiful too.' She looks towards Veeda. 'It is all thanks to my wonderful daughter, Veeda.' Veeda smiles and looks down at her hands.

After tea, Catherine Rose brings us up to date with what has been happening in Tasmania. She transports herself back to the day her father died:

He is in his 70s. It is one of those typical Tasmanian winter mornings. The sun has warmed the verandah but, below them, in the valley, the mist still clings to the ground awaiting the sun's burn off. He is sitting in his chair with his beloved

Rasna beside him in the rocker.

He has just been holding court on warfare tactics employed by the British in India and Tasmania. His audience, the twins, James Jnr. and Edgar are on their regular visit to check on their parent's welfare. They sit, as they have done all their lives, on the verandah steps looking up at their father. Catherine Rose is inside making tea but she listens to the wise words. As he speaks of war, she is reminded of the day her Papa said 'Catherine Rose, as a woman, you are a warrior fighting an unfair war. Be brave'. She is also reminded of the war fought by Truganini and her people.

He explains how the successful warfare tactics employed by Hannibal, deemed the father of warfare strategy, and later, Napoleon who followed Hannibal's tactics, were based on the observation of animals in the wild.

'Lions,' he says 'in the wild, employ the practice of fanning out and partially encircling their prey, cutting off potential escape routes. They stalk their prey, staying within 100 m of them before rushing them.' After a sip of his morning cuppa, he continues,

'The Zulus in Africa employed these same tactics. The cow horn technique resulted in the encirclement and easy destruction of their enemies. King Shaka, the Zulu warrior developed this technique in the early 1800s. He recognised the importance also of selecting the right topography, the hills and tall grass which facilitated the effectiveness of the technique.' Another sip of his tea and he continues,

'In India, tiger hunting in the 1800s involved Hunquah. Fire was lit. Beaters, men with sticks, drove fleeing animals into netting and once trapped, packs of hunting dogs were released. The tigers were shot. This was not sport, it was considered necessary to protect the local people. The tigers were responsible for the deaths of many villagers.'

He pauses, deep in thought 'weather was also considered an important factor in success.'

'A combination of these tactics was the basis of the Black Line campaign here in Tasmania.'

He shakes his head, 'What happened was inevitable. They failed to take into account the harsh topography and the inclement weather they encountered. More importantly, they failed to recognise that those being hunted were not animals but humans. Thankfully, the Aboriginals easily escaped the trap. They were familiar with the land and the weather conditions whilst the hunters were not, and they became trapped in the impenetrable forests and hills during sleet and snowfall.'

He looks down at his hands, in sorrow he continues, 'The Aboriginals may have escaped then but they could not escape the destruction of their environment which took away their life support systems which had maintained them for thousands of years. This destruction also led to their vulnerability to diseases brought in by foreign invaders. The lesson is that we must always acknowledge that we are dependent, like the animals, upon our environment for our

survival. I hope future Tasmanians appreciate this and will protect the land to ensure the survival of future generations.'
As light rain begins to fall, he looks towards the heavens and says,
'Send her down, Huey.'
His sons look at one another. They smile.
'Yes, send her down, Huey.'
James Jnr. continues on point, 'Yes, Papa, we will remind them whenever the land is threatened with destruction.'
They get up from their familiar place at the foot of their father, and go inside for more tea and biscuits. Their father attempts to raise himself from his chair. He grabs his beloved Rasna's hand. He slumps back. She raises her head from her chest, and focuses on those fading almandine eyes which stare into hers.
'I love you James,' she says and resumes her dreams.
It is James Jnr. who finds his father has passed on. The doctor is called. It was his heart that failed. Not his spirit.

Catherine Rose continues her story. My Grandma Rasna, having grown frail of late, suffers the effects of dementia. Her short term memory is impaired. Catherine Rose places the pink knitted rug with embroidered butterflies and bees over her mother's legs and wraps the soft velvet patchwork shawl around her shoulders. These had been crafted by Catherine Rose for her dear Mama during her years of isolation. Creative pursuits had helped her cope with the physical and psychological pain of her damaged face.

My Grandpa was buried in the local church cemetery. He was well regarded. His funeral was attended by several hundred members of the local community.

'A life well lived,' said the preacher. 'He was a kind, humble man, of high moral values. He saw his duty as helping those he came into contact with. He treated neighbours as family and he was much loved by all who knew him. His wisdom will be missed. His memory will live on.'

After the wake held at the Community Hall next to the Church, Catherine Rose takes Grandma Rasna home. The old lady sits, looking at the empty chair. His glasses rest on top of the last books he was reading. One was on Suess' Gondwana region in Central India and the Proto-Australoid population wave of migration. The other was on the Government's White Australia policy.

In a moment of clarity, the old lady says, 'we will meet again dear James, in heaven.'

That evening, she calls out. Catherine Rose goes to her.

'Rose, is that you?'

'It is Catherine Rose, Mama.'

'Rose? Yes, I buried Aunty Banita . I kept my promise. She was not burnt like our dear mother and you, my darling sister. I made sure that didn't happen, Rose.'

There is a pause. She slumbers. She wakes. Her eyes are clear. Looking at Catherine Rose she says with excitement.

'I can see you Rose. Yes, I see Aunty Banita and our mother and yes, I see my dear children Aarchie Lucille and

Elizabeth. You all wait for me.' She continues as if responding to questions. 'Yes mother, I will join you soon and you can tell me about your life.' The old lady pauses. She is listening to voices in heaven. 'Yes mama, out of remorse, Papa could never speak your name. Rose? Yes, I will make sure the music box passes to the girls of the family. Yes, Rose, *Giselle* still dances.'

Her dear Mama died the following day. She was buried with her beloved James.

Catherine Rose rises and hugs my Papa and Mama. She takes the pink music box from her bag. 'Faded it may be,' she says as she unwraps it from the protective packing, 'but it still works.' She winds the small key twice. Up pops *Giselle*. The music plays for a short time. Catherine Rose closes the box. 'Mama told me to pass the music box to the next girl born to the family. My mama takes the precious gift and puts it away safely. 'This is your birthday present Beryl.'

It is 1931. I am fifteen years old. The older I get the more I resent my sister Vivian. My Papa favours her. She does what she likes. She argues with him and stays out late with her boyfriend. She wears lots of makeup. She is very popular with boys. I don't go out. I have to gather grass from the school yard in the afternoons for the horse and help in our shop opposite the local school. I help Mama make pies and chips for the school kid's lunches. After school I have to help in the shop. The kids buy icy blocks and lollies. I do not have any friends.

Papa takes the horse and cart around the neighbourhood selling vegetables. Mama and I are glad he is away most of the day. He is always angry. Mama says it is because his feet hurt. When he was in Tasmania he got a fever after he went out in a bad storm to bring in the cows. His feet are deformed. He has to wear special boots so that he can walk. He still shows off by lifting Vivian on the end of the shovel. Mama says he changed after he got sick. It didn't help when he couldn't go to war to help save Britain. His mates joined up and came back as war heroes. Mama says a lot of young men did not come back so he should have been glad he couldn't go.

His only joy these days is horse racing. He goes down the road to his SP bookie every Saturday afternoon with the day's takings and places bets. He comes home and sits by the radio. Mama and I keep busy in the shop getting things ready for Monday. We listen for the results of the race, not from the radio but from Papa's reactions. It is obvious when he has won or lost from the words that flow.

The blessing, Mama says, is that he doesn't drink like some men and come home and belt up his wife and kids. Mama is a Methodist. She doesn't abide drinking. She says, 'lips that touch liquor shall never touch mine'. Vivian says, 'Well, they've touched mine Mama' and laughs.

I have a job cleaning the floors of the local funeral parlour. I have applied for a job at the local milk bar opposite the cinema. Papa is angry. 'No daughter of mine is going to work in a milk bar with those *ruffians* eyeing her off.'

Mama speaks quietly to him pointing out the need to feed the family. The job will pay more than the one I already have. Vivian goes to work each day selling hats to wealthy ladies in the city. She does not give anything to Mama but spends it on her own clothes and train fares. 'I have to dress well to keep my job' she says. My brother Kenneth works as a labourer. He does not earn much but what he does, he gives to Mama. He likes wrestling. He enters competitions each weekend. He practices the holds on me. Last night I suffered through the 'Half Nelson' in the hope that he will win his next match and collect the prize money for Mama.

Fragments of a Life

Coupling and uncoupling, war, domestic violence, incest, infanticide, institutional abuse. The vulnerable, women and children, suffer. The butterfly does not have any defence mechanism. It depends upon the strength of its hard outer case however, once it emerges from the chrysalis, it lives at the whim of its environment. The wonder is that as a species it has survived. The bee, the social altruist, knows survival depends on the survival of the Queen. The Queen guarantees the future of the community. And so it is with the human species.

Rosetta

South Sydney. New South Wales

It is 1949. My name is Rosetta. I am five years old today. I wake to the sound of my father Donald and my mother Beryl calling me into the big bed. Through sleepy eyes I see presents on the bed. I see pink tissue paper and a birthday card with a clown on it. I keep looking at his big red nose. I jump up on the bed and my father says 'Well, come on birthday girl, open the presents, I haven't got all day, I've got to get to work and you have to go to school.' He gives me a big kiss and says, 'Have a good day skeeta.' 'Don't call me that,' I say, 'I'm not a mosquito'. Mother and I read the card together, 'To dear Rosetta with love from mummy and daddy'. It doesn't take much to tear open the tissue paper. A pair of red rain boots. They aren't the black ones I wanted. 'You'll be able to wear them to school today because it's raining.' I open the other present. Five hankies with cartoon characters on them, wrapped in cellophane. 'Thanks mum, I like the hankies.' We cuddle back under the covers. I ask her to tell me again about the day I was born. 'It was Mother's Day when the nurse brought you from the nursery and I held you in my arms for the first time and cried.' 'Why did you cry? I look up at her and see a tear spilling down her cheek. 'Your daddy was away at the war when you were born and I had been very lonely but now I had you, my own little girl to cuddle, so they were happy tears.' My mother holds me so tight I can't breathe so I push away. 'Tell me again what the nurse said when I was born. 'Well, shortly after you were born the Army boss told your daddy that it was very important for him to be with us.' When your daddy entered our room all the nurses started to laugh. One said, 'Well there's no doubting who the father of this child is.' 'Why did she say that, mum?' 'Well, darling, because you looked just like daddy. Your hair was as black as coal, just like his, and you had very long legs for a baby so we knew you would be tall just like him.' I smiled and hugged her and said, 'Don't cry mum, it's my birthday. I have to get ready for school.' I run to my bed where my clothes are laid out. I don't want to wear the red rain boots but my mother insists. I don't want to make her cry again so I wear them.

On the school bus the other kids all laugh at my red boots. They all wear black boots. Thankfully, once I reach the school room we are all required to remove our boots and leave them outside. I look like everyone else. I have my white socks like everyone else. I have one of my new hankies, the one with Bambi on it, pinned to my school uniform. We are sitting in rows on the floor in front of the teacher. She is old, like my Nana, and the skin on her arm waves at me as she points to the story book we are reading. I accidentally push the boy sitting next to me and he punches me in the nose. I cry as the blood starts to drip on my uniform. Miss Hatfield stops reading and drags the boy to the naughty corner. She then unpins my new hankie and holds it tightly against my nose until the bleeding stops. For some reason, the other kids decide they like the boy better than me and no one comes to sit with me at recess or lunch time. Because it is raining heavily we remain inside so I don't have to put on the red boots until the bell rings at 3 o'clock. I wait until all the other kids have left before I put on the boots and I dawdle my way to the gate where my mother and Nana are waiting. 'What happened to you?' says Nana Maudie. 'A boy punched me in the nose, Nana' and my mother says 'Where's your hankie?' I take it from my pocket. 'Sorry, mum, I got blood on it.' 'Oh, don't worry, it'll wash out.' Nana says 'Why did he hit you? and I say 'He doesn't like girls.' 'Oh', says Nana 'I bet that changes in a few years' time' and she starts to giggle her famous giggle and I say, 'Don't laugh at me Nana, I've had a bad day.' 'Sorry Rosetta , I'm not laughing at you, I'm laughing at the silly boy who hit you.'

We sit on the bus seat. Nana lifts me up on her generous lap as my mother tries to wipe away the blood and the muddy tears from my face. I try to avoid the pain and in so doing, I start to slide down Nana's bulging body. Once on the ground I regain my balance and take off along the path with my mother closely behind me. We return to the bus stop just in time to board the bus for the trip home. Things improve once we are home. There is a sponge birthday cake with mock cream in the middle and white icing on top. My name *Rosetta* is piped in pink icing on the top. A plate of fairy bread with hundreds and thousands on it and orange cordial waiting. Five pink birthday candles are placed around my name and lit. My Nana and my mother sing Happy Birthday to me as I blow out the candles. I say 'Can we save some cake and candles for daddy?' 'Of course, but you know he won't be home until after its dark and you will be asleep by then.'

It is 1954. I am ten years old today. A lot has happened in the last five years. I remember the day the boy I liked at school, Brian Jamison, BJ for short, pushed me in the bushes because I tried to walk too close to him on the way to the bus stop after school. I had a lot of sore throats and I would have high fevers when my tonsils became infected. One night I was feverish and called to my mother for a drink of water. I sat up in bed and whispered 'BJ's in the room, mum'. The next day my mother told me that I was very sick during the night and was delirious and imagined BJ was in the room.

   I remember the day my mother and father didn't kiss anymore. After that there were many times when my mother would pack a few clothes into a string bag and we would go to stay with Nana Maudie and Poppa Willie. I went to a different school. The children liked me there. My red rain boots by then were long gone but as my mother had predicted, everyone was wearing red rain boots by then and the black ones I had insisted on were now old fashioned. My mother was working at a milk bar and I would spend time with my father on weekends. On one of these times a strange lady came to visit and stayed the night in the big bed. I told my mother about the lady with pimples on her face who slept in the big bed. She was very upset.

We returned to live with my father. My mother got a job in a factory making sandshoes. We had to get up early in the morning when it was dark and catch the bus to the factory. Across the road was a church hall where they taught ballet and I would stay there until it was time to go to school and the ballet teacher would put me on the school bus in the mornings and collect me off the bus in the afternoons. It would be dark when we got home and the lights would be out because of the blackouts. Mum would say, 'No electricity left for us tonight'. My mother and I would just go to bed until the lights came on. One night a bat flew into the bedroom. We hid under the blankets. When my father came home he got rid of the bat. We ate when the lights came on.

I remember the day the string bag was packed with clothes and I thought we were going once again to Nana and Poppa's house. This time we went to a strange man's house. I stayed in this pretty pink bedroom. In the morning I called out for my mother and found her in a big bed. She looked lovely. She was wearing a pink satin nightie and her hair was in curling pins. She said 'How would you like to live in this house?' This man liked my mother and he took mum and I, together with his two daughters who lived with their mother, to pantomimes in the city. 'Ok' was my reply. After a few weeks my mother told me he wanted to marry her but that he had said that I reminded him all the time of my father. We went back to live with my father. My mother still cried a lot and she suffered from bad migraine headaches. I would go into her bedroom and bring her a wet face cloth and place it on her forehead. My father was angry and silent most of the time.

I remember when my mother went into hospital for an operation. She had her appendix removed and the doctor fixed a hole, I think it was in her tummy. I think she got it when I was born.

I remember the day she told me she was having a baby.

This came as a shock because for years I had been nagging her for a baby sister so I could be like my best friend Beverley. I hated being an only child. My father was happy when my brother was born. I was disappointed that it wasn't a girl but I have learned to love my brother. I was able to take him for walks in the stroller and look after him and feed him. I am happier than I have ever been and I don't care if my parents are happy or not.

It is 1959. I am fifteen years old. My Poppa Willie passed away in May. I have been staying with my Nana Maudie. My Aunty Vivian arranged for me to stay with Nana because Nana was sad and lonely. I did not want to go until mum told me that if I did, it would help the family financially. Another child, a daughter, followed shortly after my brother's birth. With two children under two years old, my mother could not work to bring in extra money. She always looked worried and she cried a lot. Her migraine headaches returned. My father spent a lot of time away. After my sister was born my mother told my father that she wanted him to leave the house because the marriage was over. The house was in her name and she thought it was best for the children. He refused to go. I went to live with my Nana Maudie.

Living with Nana Maudie is calm and quiet. She tells me about the family ancestors in Tasmania. She also tells me about my mother and father.

My father was given compassionate leave from the Army to be with my mother when I was born. After my birth he returned to the defence line formed west of Brisbane in anticipation of the feared invasion of the Japanese from the north. My mother and father had lived in Warwick in Queensland. When she knew she was pregnant she returned to live with her parents, Maudie and Willie to await my birth. Like many women, following the birth, she suffered post-natal depression. For a year she lived in isolation, afraid to venture outside the home. She spent her days listening to the radio, obsessed with the war and a husband's infidelity. My Aunty Vivian, who was married and had two sons, arranged for my mother to receive shock treatment. My Nana tells me my mother didn't remember a lot about her treatment, but she remembered the day she felt better. She was walking in the hospital garden. For the first time in a long time she was able to appreciate the beauty of nature. The roses were more beautiful than she remembered. The butterflies more wonderful. She studied the plants which attracted them. Nana says the butterfly became her inspiration to transform herself.

Being with my Nana Maudie has revived my memories of the time when my grandparents were my carers. I remember sitting on my Poppa Willie's knee by the fire, as he told me stories of Tasmania. His big blue eyes widened as he described driving the horse and cart home at night with the devils following along behind, their eyes glowing in the dark. I asked him, 'Were they blue?'

He laughed and picked up his squeeze box and started to play my favourite song 'I loves you but your feets too big.' I would blow into the tin whistle as I watched his big black boot tap in time to the music.

Everyone in the family was scared of Poppa. I was not. He was kind and loving to me. He loved the things I loved, music and flowers. We would go into the garden and he would make me posies of tiny pink roses, angel's breath and maidenhair fern.

When eventually my father returned from the Army we moved into a house not far from them. I remember our house was tiny and there was only one bedroom. There was no front door. I slept in the hallway outside the bathroom. The house was built by my Uncle Kenneth's friends who worked in the building industry. The land had been purchased from the money my father sent home during the war. Our next door neighbours lived in an old train carriage so my dad had said 'We should be grateful that we have a proper roof over our heads' but he complains that the house was not built properly. My mum says 'Well, they did the best they could.' She would remind him of the day that my Poppa Willie supported the timber roof frame on his back whilst the others put support beams in place before it crashed to the ground.

My resemblance to my father was a cause of grief for my mother. He was tall and slim and had black hair and fair skin. His heritage was English and Scottish. He was an only child. His mother died when he was thirteen. She suffered from epilepsy and suffocated during an epileptic fit. He found her on the kitchen floor when he returned from school. His father died when he was twenty from a heart attack.

I heard my mother say to a neighbour that if and when she had other children they wouldn't look like my father. He was her sister Vivian's friend. This made him acceptable to her father who had vetted all her previous boyfriends. The resentment she felt towards her sister and her father grew. 'They even chose my husband', she would say.

I recall my Aunty Vivian took me to the ballet to see *Giselle* when I was about nine years old. I had been learning ballet. Before going to the theatre in the city she took me to the big David Jones department store and I left wearing a new pink dress, new shoes and a small white handbag. When we arrived home my mother was furious. I remember the argument. I don't remember the ballet.

Today, when I get off the school bus near Nana's house I can see her sitting on the bench under the willow holding a large glass of bright red cordial for me. As I get closer, I can see she is crying. 'What's wrong Nana?' 'Rosetta, your mum came to see me today. She wants you back home because your Aunty Vivian lied and said you would not be staying in the bedroom where your Poppa passed away. I am sorry Rosetta, I did not think that would be a problem.' My father arrived in the car and I was driven home. I left school shortly after. My teachers were very upset because I was a good student. My father made me stand and watch as he burnt my school books. It was my mother's decision that I leave school. 'We cannot afford for you to stay at school. We need the money.'

It is 1965. I am twenty one today. A celebration is taking place at home tonight. A large key, crafted in Tasmanian Rosewood by a neighbour who is a French Polisher is presented to me by my mother and father. I am welcomed to adulthood. In the centre of the dining table is a cake. It is iced white. My name 'Rosetta' is engraved in pink icing. There are iced butterflies placed around its edges. The twenty one candles are set alight. I blow them out, eventually. I taste my first Champagne. I go to bed happy that I am now of age. As I close my eyes, I enter that other world:

You know she is a vision from the future, but for you she is in the present. She holds the pink music box. She has curls the colour of honey. Her eyes are blue. She tells you she has her father's nose and her mother's high cheek bones. She is tall like you. Seated beside her is her son. He has dark skin, brown eyes and black curls. She says he is the child she always desired. There is another child. A girl. Also greatly desired. She has fair skin, her eyes are blue and she has her mother's blonde hair. She is the other side of the same coin. They sit together, smiling for the camera. There is a woman with them in the photograph. It is me.

Fragments of a Life

The search for identity continues. Violence inflicted upon children imprints a value which can last a lifetime. It changes who they were supposed to be. If the chrysalis is damaged, so also the emerging butterfly? The foetus is sensitive to its external conditions. What happens to the mother has consequences for the child.

Rosetta

North Shore, Sydney. New South Wales

It is 1972. I am twenty eight years old. I have just given birth to the daughter I saw in a vision all those years ago. It was a difficult pregnancy and birth. My husband of four years is a violent man and I have left him on numerous occasions.

Finding somewhere to run to without inflicting a violent man on friends and family is the main reason I always return and of course, I want to believe his declarations that there will be no more abuse. His promises have never been honoured and the physical violence escalated until I became pregnant. The physical violence ceased during my pregnancy but was replaced with draconian rules of behaviour and mental and emotional abuse. I had, with my husband's consent, opened an employment agency for legal secretarial staff before becoming pregnant. It was a successful business. It gave me value. I was able to have a sense of independence. But during my pregnancy, my husband took over the running of the business. He resigned from his job and has seized control of the money. I have worked from home, finding the job vacancies from the classifieds and ringing the law firms and offering to find staff. I also maintain contact with established clientele and the girls who have sought employment in the past. He rings me constantly to monitor my behaviour and whereabouts. He leaves me with no money. I do not have a car. I rarely see my family. He tells me that my share of the income is in an account in my name but I do not have the details of the account. I am a prisoner. The issue of children had been raised before our marriage and my husband knew my desire for children and he had shown a willingness, notwithstanding that he was 41 years old and I was 23 years old when we married. We agreed to wait for one year before trying for a baby. The year came and went and each time I raised the question I was told 'No, you are not subservient enough to be a good mother.'

The violent outbursts started on our honeymoon. I was in shock from then on. I was embarrassed to admit to my family and friends that I had married a man who abused me. I hid the bruises and the pain. I eventually believed that I deserved to be mistreated, that it was my fault. I remember early on, saying to him that we should separate because I was not capable of making him happy because he found fault with me all the time. He just said 'No, you'll change.' I remember one violent outburst in particular. It led to my leaving him. I had mistakenly given him the half grilled tomato with the core instead of the half without the core with his bacon and eggs. He threw the plate with the offending tomato at the wall and chased me through the house. I was, by that time, practiced in avoiding him and took refuge in the bathroom, the only room with a lock on the door. When he went to work I packed a bag and left. I booked into a boarding house by the harbour so I could continue to go to work as a legal secretary in the CBD. I sought legal advice on separation and divorce. I was advised that the law required that I prove my husband's cruelty or infidelity or separate and wait five years for a divorce. I had hidden the abuse from friends and family and had never approached the police so relying on the evidence of others would be difficult and I did not have any evidence of his infidelity.

The legal office where I worked was in a very old building

down near the Quay. The female toilets were located on alternative floors. One day, on my way to the ladies toilet, my husband was hiding in the stairwell and grabbed me from behind and I was dragged down the stairs as he wrenched my wedding and engagement rings from my finger. My employer and the other staff were scared and I was embarrassed. There was no thought of calling the police. My employer, a practicing Christian, urged me to go to see the Minister who married us to see what I should do about my violent marriage. 'Divorce is never the answer' was the Minister's advice. 'You must go back and work on your marriage.' I did not consider this an option until I discovered I was three month's pregnant. I knew it was impossible for me to leave him. I had no money and my family was frightened of my husband. I knew that the child would be considered his property, as I was, and he would do all he could to keep the child from me. When I told my employer I had returned to my husband and I was pregnant he expressed joy and said I had made the right choice.

I look down at this miracle. My darling daughter. She has had a difficult entry into the world, a forceps delivery. The marks of the forceps are visible on each tiny temple. She is in isolation to allow her to recover. I am not allowed to hold her or feed her. My milk is delayed and I am put on a breast pump to encourage its flow. It is painful and my tears flow but my milk wont. My husband was not present at the birth. My obstetrician, on my initial consultation, told me he did not allow husband's into the birth suite. I was glad. I knew my husband would be critical of my efforts. I never did anything right. He is not here now. I know he will be in shock. He expected a son.

I lie here, in a room of new mothers with their babies happily feeding. Their loving partners, friends and family arrive with flowers and gifts. My mother, who is now widowed, spent the final days of my pregnancy at my home but when I went to hospital she was immediately driven home to her house by my husband. I am alone. I spent most of yesterday sitting outside the nursery looking at my lovely baby daughter through glass. Today I woke up angry. I went to the public phone at the end of the corridor. I rang a local florist. I ordered a large 'pink floral arrangement' to be delivered to me. The card chosen bears butterflies and reads, 'To Rosetta's baby girl. Welcome. With love always.' I charged it to the business. I am looking at it now with my baby in my arms.

He frightened me this morning. Protecting my body had been paramount. This morning I am frightened for my baby daughter's body.

In the last few weeks he has changed. During my pregnancy he didn't hit me. He found other ways to control me. He fed me with highly spiced food. He took over my business. He stopped me having control of my money. He stopped me from using the car. Now he pushes me away. He keeps me from my daughter. I can still see him holding her above his head on the balcony. He was showing off to the guests assembled after her christening. I'm scared. I look down at my hands. They are clenched. Pressed into my stomach. I look in the mirror. Unshed tears have created welts around my eyes. My lips tremble. Physically I am ready to throw up. It's not fear for myself any more. It's fear for her. I know how to limit his abuse towards me. Don't fight back. Go silent. Lock yourself in the bathroom until he calms down or leaves the house. But how do I protect her?

When he got home last night he kicked over the drying frame with baby clothes on it. 'Get that shit out of the lounge room.' He grabbed her from my arms and took her into her room and undressed her. She woke during the night. I went to her. He grabbed her and jogged up and down in the hall for about an hour until she went to sleep. This morning he brought her into our bed. He stripped and had a shower in the ensuite. She was lying on his side of the bed. He came out naked and leaned over her.

I've got to escape. I need a plan.

It is July 1973. It is the first birthday of my daughter Melody Rose. Her present from mummy is a pink music box. There is a ballerina who dances when music plays. I remember my mother Beryl had one and I loved it. I was not allowed to play with it. I don't know what happened to it. My mother, my brother Kenny and my sister Sonja live next door to me and my daughter. We have rented two units on the sixth floor of a new high rise apartment block in the western suburbs of Sydney. My mother sold the family home. My father suffered a massive heart attack and died at the age of fifty one. Sadly, he did not live to see me free from my violent husband or to meet his granddaughter. I was granted a divorce on the grounds of cruelty. My husband chose not to defend the petition. By consent, we also reached a property settlement. This was conditional upon him having access to our daughter and payment of maintenance. Initially, I had rejected any form of access because of his actions whilst we were separated. The legal advice still rings in my ears 'Agree so that you can have money to buy a home for you and your daughter and obtain your divorce. You will be free of him. You cannot fight the case because you do not have very good evidence of cruelty. It will be your word against his. If the case goes to Court you may lose.' The amount agreed was calculated on the basis that I was young and the statistics showed that I would remarry within three years. I remain a chattel, dependent upon the goodwill of a husband. The money I received is insufficient to purchase a small unit outright.

My mind goes back to that day in January 1973 when I escaped the violence. Melody is six months old. That morning I stood looking down at her as she slept in her cot. She is an innocent born into a nightmare I thought. Her innocence was broken last night when he hit me in front of her. The physical abuse resumed once I was home with the baby. A further source of abuse was added, that involving my daughter. He would grab her from my arms and withhold her from me until I conceded to his demands. I know I have to leave. I know it must be today. During the last six months I have been planning how to get away. I have located the details of the bank account in which he has been placing the takings from my business. It is in my name and I am the signatory. He says this is only to save on tax. He is running the office and I am still working from home. He thinks I am too afraid to go anywhere let alone use the money banked in my name. I am not. I know I must do this for my daughter. I have a source of funds now. I can escape. I just have to plan how to do it and where to go. Christmas is over and he is going into the office today. I ask him to leave the car because I have to take the baby for a medical check-up. He agrees. I pack a bag with our clothes. I take the umbrella stroller. I drive into the city and park the car in Pitt Street. I go to the Bank and withdraw all the money from the account in my name and open a new account in my daughter's name at another Bank. I am the Trustee on the account so I can withdraw the funds. I go to the airline booking office nearby and purchase a flight to Adelaide. I use a different name. During the flight to Adelaide, one of the airline hostesses says, 'You should go further, go to Perth.' I am surprised. 'Why?' 'It is a great place for single men' but I reply, 'No, I am going to Adelaide because I hear it is a great place for single mothers.' I spend time during the flight reading articles in Cleo. They give me hope. My darling girl giggles and plays with the hostesses. It is hot when we reach Adelaide at about 8 o'clock at night. I have not booked any accommodation. I want to make it difficult for him to trace my whereabouts. I go to the taxi rank and ask the driver to take me to the nearest accommodation suitable for myself and my baby. I end up in a hotel room at a pub at Glenelg. It is Friday night. The sound of the rock and roll music below me keeps me awake for hours but eventually Melody falls asleep despite the noise. Exhausted, I eventually sleep until the morning sun blasts through the windows on my first day of freedom from abuse.

I feed Melody and eat breakfast at a cafe looking out at the ocean. Melody is happy in the stroller and I walk to the end of the pier. When the shops open I go and buy a local paper with house to let classifieds. I see a garden flat advertised. It is just around the corner from the shopping centre. I ring. It is suitably furnished. It has two bedrooms. A lovely garden suitable for a child brings tears to my eyes as I image Melody playing safely in the sunshine. An hour later I have the key and I spend another hour purchasing a cot and high chair and other baby needs. I walk along the street with my baby girl. I feel like another person, someone who is free. All of a sudden I feel someone looking at me. I put my head down. I look around. I expect to see my husband, his angry face, his clenched fist, running towards me. He isn't there. 'Not free yet,' I say to myself.

The house has been divided into two flats. There is a family living in the front flat. As I walk past the front flat the next day, a middle aged woman comes out of the front door and welcomes me. She is about my mother's age. I confide in her that I have escaped a violent husband. She then confides in me. She has been in a violent marriage for twenty five years. She shows me a bruise on her upper arm which is covered by her shirt. 'You have done the right thing. Don't go back, you hear.' She comes over to me, and whispers 'I wasn't able to leave my husband once I had the children. He always threatened to kill me and the children if I left. I couldn't risk it. Anyway, I had nowhere to go. The children left as soon as they could cope on their own. They don't speak to me now because they don't understand why I stay. But where can I go? I have lost everything. I hate him and I hate myself. I don't think I could support myself. I haven't worked for years and I have no friends or family to help me.' I give her the Cleo from my bag 'Here. It has an article on how to leave.' She hides it under her shirt. She points towards the house. 'He's here now. I can't let him see it.' She turns as she hurries into the house. 'Good luck to you and your baby.'

I write a letter to my mother. I tell her where I am and that we are ok. I say I managed to escape whilst I was still alive. My mother tells the Police of my whereabouts. Two female constables arrive at my flat. They say they will not divulge my whereabouts. They are here to satisfy my family that I am safe. My mother says that my husband has told her that I am suicidal and she must disclose my whereabouts because I may harm his daughter.

I consult a lawyer in Adelaide. The first thing I insist upon is that they do not disclose my whereabouts. I tell the lawyer my husband is violent. They agree. I appear in Court seeking an injunction to prevent my husband from selling the home in Sydney which is in his name only. The injunction is granted. My husband is to be served. My solicitor assures me that I will be protected. I am not. The document served on my husband discloses my address but I do not know this.

I remember the knock on the door. I had just put Melody to bed. It had been a lovely day. I was feeling positive having had weeks of peace and quiet. My body feels like it belongs to me. It's not under attack. I open the door with a smile, it is probably my neighbour with some scones again. He stands there on the other side of the flimsy flyscreen door. He opens it and pushes his way in and says 'Where's my daughter? If you have harmed her, I'll kill you.' He wakes her up and dances around the room. I am numb. He returns her to her cot. She is crying and screams for an hour. He won't let me comfort her. 'I'll make it all ok. We will have another baby, a boy this time, and you'll be able to get back to your old self. I know you are just suffering post natal depression. We'll get you to a doctor tomorrow. He can put you back on Valium.' He's on top of me. He tears off my clothes and rapes me.

I don't even scream. I am dead inside. I pray. 'Please God, don't make me pregnant.'

In the morning he shows me his feet. He has blisters on his heels. 'Thanks to you I had to walk miles yesterday trying to find you.' I need to get to a chemist and then to book some flights home.' I dress and feed Melody. I am crying inside but I am determined that I will never go back to him. I agree to go to the shops with him to find a chemist and a travel agent. I take a bag with baby formula and nappies and we head off. Melody is in the stroller. When we get to the chemist I say I have to change the baby's nappy. I head towards the toilet and baby change room. He says he will stay and buy the band aids he needs. I close the door behind me I know there is a back door. I push the stroller through the door and I am gone. I head for the main road. I see a tram. I jump aboard. I go into a cafe in the city. I look up Karitane Toddler Clinics. I find their address. I have no one I know in Adelaide. I need to find a safe place for my daughter. I need to know that she will be cared for and protected, no matter what happens to me. I explain my difficulties and the fact that I have nowhere to go. They book Melody in for their sleep and settling program. I am able to stay there, but I choose to book into a motel nearby. I don't want her to be with me whilst he is searching for me. I wait until Melody is settled and asleep and I head to the motel. I ring the solicitor. I find out how my husband located me. 'An oversight,' he says. His legal advice 'I think you ought to go back to your family in Sydney so you can sort things out with your husband without having to go to Court.' I keep on saying, 'but he raped me, doesn't that matter?' Apparently not.

I am back in Sydney with Melody. A girl friend has collected us from the airport. We go to her office in Australia Square in the centre of Sydney. She is on the 37th level. She rings a solicitor she knows. I make an appointment to see him. The phone rings. It is my husband. Clearly he knows my whereabouts. He says he understands that the marriage is over. He will agree to the divorce and to a property settlement. He wants to see me and Melody. I do not agree. I hang up. My friends encourage me to just meet with him. They ring and he comes to the office. He asks them if he can speak to me privately and they leave. I have Melody on my lap. He grabs her, and runs out of the office. I scream. 'He's got the baby.' We all run out to the foyer and to the lifts. He isn't there. We press buttons and run around in a panic. Someone goes to the fire stairs. He is running down the stairs with the baby. There are 39 levels in Australia Square. We call the police. They arrive too late. He's gone. The baby's gone. I am whisked away to my friend's home. Her husband suggests 'A stiff drink is what you need.' I gulp down a mouthful of Scotch whisky. I immediately bring it up and spend the whole night vomiting and crying over the toilet. In the morning my friend arranges an appointment with the solicitor. The legal situation is that my husband has the right to do what he has done. There is no official Court order which would deny him custody of our daughter. The only order is the injunction on the sale of the house obtained in Adelaide. I go back home to my mother's house. She does not have a home phone so I spend many hours yelling into the public phone across the road. It is the western suburbs of Sydney in February. I am getting thinner and thinner, sadder and sadder. We don't know where Melody is. The police tell us that he has refused to say where the baby is. She is only seven months old. Everyone is concerned but no one seems to be able to force him to return her. My friend contacts me. He isn't operating the business. She suggests that I ring him and tell him he can keep the baby and that I will take back the business. I am shocked at the suggestion but I am desperate so I do it. It works. He agrees to return the baby to me at her office. As he hands her over to me he places a brown paper bag on the desk and says 'You haven't won, bitch' and walks out.

My friend opens the package. It is my daughter's little potty and it has faeces in it. 'He is sick in the head' says my friend.

I crawl away with my baby.

Fragments of a Life

As I re-enter this body, I am met with a heart, broken and shattered like an unlucky mirror. Through the shards of disappointment and loss, a spirit lives and a soul is replenished through the love of self. It is reflected in her eyes. The chrysalis, the home, which has bound the butterfly to this earth and provided it with nurture during its metamorphosis, detaches. She is ready to face a new beginning. A life yet to be. For a short time she will be free to be herself. The consequences of this freedom are grave. Separation from family and loved ones. Guilt for perceived crimes and misdemeanours. Expectations not met. The butterfly welcomes metamorphosis. It knows the ending at the beginning of a new life. Women experience a new beginning with each child's birth.

Rosetta
Sunshine Coast. Queensland

I awake this morning from a night filled with terror. Flashbacks invade my sleeping hours. I wake exhausted having relived moments I would rather forget. Since my close encounter with death, I revisit the past every night. It's like I'm drowning in a sea of memories. I'm in a hurry not to forget anything and to question everything. The accuracy of my memory. Did that really happen to me? Did I really say and do that? Who was I then? It feels like it happened to another person. I resolve, it did, it happened to the person I used to be. Who am I now? I look down at my arm. It is the arm of a woman in her seventies. The hand attached to this arm bears a bulging road map of pulsating blood leading to my heart. The bones show through like yellowed piano keys. They play out of tune. The worn out skin, flecked with scars from the sun, reflect the scars on my heart. I lay here, alone. On the bedside table is a photo of a younger version of me. I hold my brand new granddaughter and my seven year old grandson sits next to me. This captured moment of happiness and joy provide me with evidence that I once was loved. They now cause me the pain of loss. Habits of a lifetime. I rise. Another day has been afforded me. I go to my desk and begin my daily prescription. Write a thousand words. The memories flow. Grist for the mill of my Master's Thesis.

It is 1973 again. I am sitting in my mother's car, my daughter Melody is on my lap. My husband is wrenching the car door open. I make an effort to lock the door. He is too fast. He leans across me and grabs at Melody. 'Give me my daughter, you bitch.' I look in his eyes and I see hatred and fear. I cling to my daughter and in the process she is dragged across the steering wheel and I scream in his face. 'Stop, you are hurting her.' He pulls away. The baby is screaming. My mother is yelling at him. 'Go away you monster, I will call the police and have you locked up.' He takes off. We drive off in the car. There is a small lump on Melody's head. The doctor says 'It's nothing to worry about.' I try to speak to him about my violent husband. He doesn't want to know. No one wants to know.

My mother and I decide we will move into some new apartments where the security will be better than it was in her home. My husband has been given access to Melody but only within the unit I now reside in. I am allowed to have another person present during his three hour access, from nine to twelve each Sunday. My mother's unit is adjacent to that of a divorced man who has heard my husband bashing on the door of my unit when he was not supposed to be there. He has a telephone. My mother and I do not. He has offered to help. He says he will come and stay during the access if necessary. He sits reading the paper. My husband demands that he leave. He refuses. My husband grabs Melody and goes out on the sixth floor balcony and holds her over the edge. The neighbour rushes out to ring the police. My mother is on the adjoining balcony. She is pleading with my husband to go inside with the baby. Eventually he comes inside and immediately takes her down in the lift and sits in the garden area with her. When I reach the garden he walks off with her. The police arrive they take the baby from him and return her to me. He keeps on saying he must be able to take her out of my unit. I go to see the local magistrate the next day. After waiting for several hours I eventually get to speak to a kindly older man who says that the safest thing in his opinion is to move away. 'Lose yourself' he says. 'I know your husband's type. He will move on to another victim and leave you alone if you disappear.' We do and he does, eventually.

Fragments of a Life

I enter a soul preparing for death. She has secrets that need to be shared. Silence has only added to the pain. The butterflies, beautiful, but encased in glass, hang on her wall. A gift from one who knew her passion. She goes to the window and searches her butterfly tree for the living treasure. Not today. There is always tomorrow.

Beryl
Sunshine Coast. Queensland

It is October 2005. I have just celebrated my 84th birthday. My granddaughter, Melody, came with gifts. My great granddaughter Lucy, dances for me. She spins around squealing with the delight only a three year old can experience. The joy of being a ballerina. As she twirls around, I remember a pink music box and another ballerina, Giselle. I remember the day I sat at the large kitchen table trying to hide the scribbling of my name on white butcher's paper. I wake each morning having reviewed my life during my sleeping hours. As if I'm drowning, I rush to relive those moments, joyful and sad, before I take my final journey. It is wartime. I am pregnant. This is a child I am determined to keep. I am married this time. No shame will attach to this birth. My husband is stationed at the Brisbane Line defences near Warwick in Queensland. I am back with my mother and father. I reopen and read again and again the letter from Mrs Mags, my neighbour in Warwick, telling me of my husband's infidelity. I cry a lot and stay in my room a lot. I am sad. I look down at my knee. My great granddaughter is gently patting me, 'Nana, watch me dance.' I am back in the moment. 'Oh, yes, my dear girl, please dance for Nana, I am watching.'

My life. It has always been about the children. I returned time and again to an unhappy marriage for the sake of the children. My husband, in a rare moment of disclosure, not long before he died, said 'I wonder if it would have been better for our marriage if we had kept that first baby.' I think he finally realised, or was prepared to acknowledge the emotional price I had paid for his decision. It was a boy. My mother knew I was pregnant. She said 'Your father will disown you.' I remember thinking, he doesn't think that highly of me anyway, but I still sought his approval. In the end though, it was not my decision. It was my husband's. He was scared of losing my father's approval. The decision to abort left me wanting a child as revenge for the one I lost.

It also left me with the need to hear my husband plead for my forgiveness of his infidelity. He never would. I remember him prone on the floor, punching the floor with his fists denying any infidelity. Revenge led to my own infidelity.

My fading eyes study my granddaughter and her daughter. They could be sisters. Same hair, golden and curly, same blue eyes. I would like to say to Melody 'You got the children you desired didn't you. One black and one white. I used to tell you I should have run away with a black man. Like me, I dreamed of the children I would have long before they arrived. Your mother, my darling Rosetta, looked like her father and you looked like your father but you grew into who you were supposed to be. Your children will grow into who they are supposed to be in spite of their mother. I tried to influence your mother's choice of husband. I hated my father and sister for choosing my husband but I finished up trying to do the same to your mother. Your poor mother was a vulnerable soul. I thought she would never be able to defend herself against the bullies. I remember watching from the kitchen window when she was about four years of age as she tried to push away a little boy who was laying on top of her. I called out to her, 'Push him off,' but she couldn't, she wasn't physically strong enough. I couldn't bear it so I rushed down and pulled him off her.

I remember her first day at school. She came home with a bloody nose. A boy had punched her because 'he didn't like girls' she said. Then later, a boy she liked pushed her in the bushes on the way to the bus stop. Of course you know your father was violent and she left when she feared he would hurt you. I was there the day he held you over the balcony six floors up. I pleaded with him to go inside. I wanted to grab a knife and kill him that day. I was still trying to protect her from bullies. I was ready to redeem my failure to warn her against your father. Your grandfather knew of your father before your mother met him. He had been engaged to his secretary. He had counselled her to break off their engagement after your father had physically abused her and her father. Your grandfather would not let me tell your mother. He feared for his own life and his family at a time when he was recovering from a heart attack.

Your mother held me tightly when I wanted to kill your father. 'Mum, its okay,' she said. 'I wont let him hurt her again.' She was physically exhausted but she relied upon her brain, she got a law degree and fought him through the Courts. 'We ran away, you know. You, your mum and I, and here you are with your own little boy and girl.

Rosa

Like lightning through the darkness of a stormy night I see so clearly my identity. Memories of past lives live within us. I am Rosa. I am the butterfly. I have weathered the storms of life. Each battered soul still harbours the memories of those who came before but each new life comes with the desire to change the world and make it a kinder place.

EPILOGUE

Biologists know the labelling of objects based on colour and gender are inventions of the human mind. Colour and gender are in the mind of the beholder. Butterflies have twelve times the colour receptors of humans. The butterfly uses colour as an aid in the collection of nectar. The importance of colour in humans is a cultural thing. It is a learned response, having been passed on through the generations. That which is taught can be modified. It can be unlearned. Through the generations, the female of the species knows that, like the butterfly, survival only comes through metamorphosis.

METAMORPHOSIS

I am the sum total of everything that went before me,
of all I have been, seen, done,
of everything done-to-me.

- **Salman Rushdie** -

My search for identity is complete

I was born in May 1944. WWII was still to find its end. Men and women and the world's children were still dying. An atomic bomb would end it but not the suffering. I was born into a private war between my mother and father. My father was the only child of a 'fine English gentleman' who was married to a 'fine Australian second generation Scottish lassie'. She lived in Goulburn in New South Wales. She became an epileptic at fourteen as a result of a bout of meningitis. She died at forty on her kitchen floor. My father found her there when he came home from school. He was thirteen. He tried to revive her as he had been taught but she was already gone. His father, a carpenter, was not comfortable without a wife. He quickly remarried to a woman who immediately dispensed with the child by making him homeless. My father went to stay with his dead mother's relatives in Sydney.

He got a job at fifteen with Shelley's in Sydney but he

became dependent upon his mother's extended family for food and a place to live. His Aunty Polly and Uncle Harry in Ashfield gave him a bed. He was often hungry and would sneak into the kitchen at night for something to eat. His father died when he was twenty of a heart attack. He was then welcomed into the home of his stepmother who charged him board and told neighbours he was her natural born son.

The story was she sold the matrimonial home on the death of his father by signing the transfer documents as his dead mother. She and his mother had the same first name. My father saw this as his inheritance having been stolen by her. It was while he lived with his stepmother that he met my mother. He was a friend of her sister. They would travel into the city on the train from Bankstown each morning. My father was tall and had a widow's peak hairline. His straight black hair would fall down onto his face and he would toss his head back in a rakish manner that impressed the ladies apparently. He was considered handsome. He resembled movie stars of the time. He was charming and had a wicked sense of humour. However, after a bout of meningitis at the age of twenty he had been left with hands that shook. My mother was not overly taken with him. She pined for a boy she used to go to the movies with until her father said he was unsuitable because 'he's got a large button hole on his overcoat.' My mother never understood the logic of this failing but accepted the loss of her choice. Because her sister approved of my father he was accepted as a fitting beau for my mother. In my mother's opinion he was a womaniser. At best a flirt who meant no harm.

Sadly my mother was to find her instincts were correct. He could be cruel. He slapped her across the face in an argument. She got pregnant and had an abortion. After the abortion they got married. She was twenty and he had been conscripted into the army. The wedding was a disaster. Years later she confessed that she had lied about her age on the marriage certificate. She was to turn twenty one in October. They married in June before my father was required to join the Army. The groom giggled through the ceremony causing the reverend in the Dulwich Hill Anglican Church to remind him and the best man of the seriousness of the occasion to be taken soberly. Both of them where greatly inebriated apparently. The wedding night disappointed the bride. Her new husband threw up all night and peed in the hand basin.

Shortly after the marriage he was stationed at the Brisbane line of defence at Warwick in Queensland. She went to visit him and stayed for several months with her new husband in a share house with a married couple from Queensland. She became pregnant and returned to live with her parents in Bankstown. More sadness when she was told by the couple in the Warwick house that my father was having an affair with an Army nurse stationed in Warwick. My mother abandoned and alone in wartime gave birth to me in St George Hospital on the 9th May 1944 just after Mother's Day. It was a difficult birth. A breach birth resulted in damage to my right hand. She also suffered internal tearing which wasn't fixed for nine years. She suffered post natal depression and did not leave her parents house for the first year of my life. Her sister took steps to arrange for her to have electric shock treatment. She recovered. She was collected from the hospital by my father who said 'Thank God I won't have to come to this hospital any more.' He returned to active duty in the islands off New Guinea. He was on a war ship when the Japanese surrendered in 1945.

When my father came home from the war, I was about eighteen months old. WWIII commenced when my mother and father cohabited. She wanted him to admit infidelity. He refused. She never forgave him. Revenge was her panacea. She had affairs. She had two children who were not my father's children. My father accepted them as his own according to the prevailing law. They were children of the marriage. I looked like my father. Tall slim and blue black hair. My brother nine years younger and my sister eleven years younger held no resemblance to my father. This was what my mother had declared years before. 'I'll have more children but they won't look like him.' She confessed these 'sins' but never regretted the result. She loved all her children.

Like the butterfly, I morphed into the real me after the birth of my daughter. A girl with strawberry blonde curls. I got brave. With my mother's support I fought back for myself and my daughter. It took courage and brainpower relying on the court system eventually. We blossomed after my ex chose to move on with another wife and child.

I enrolled in an Arts Law degree having been accepted under a mature aged entry into UNSW in 1979. Sadly, after five years of normalisation, my ex re-entered our lives. He sought custody of my daughter. I had enrolled my daughter as a boarder in a Private School. She had developmental problems. She was not able to run without tripping because she lacked balance and was falling behind in reading and writing skills. Doctors I had consulted said I was just a nervous mother. My mother said that was nonsense. She had raised three children and my daughter was the only one who couldn't catch a ball thrown to her at five years of age.

We discovered the reason for the ex's sudden desire to have custody. My ex and his then wife had lost a child, a daughter, at birth. I was worried about my daughter's safety. I hoped my daughter would improve at the School as they anticipated to me she would. My daughter did not do well as a boarder. She told me on the first visit home that staff and students were unkind to her. The staff acknowledged she was having problems and was not improving academically. She returned to my new home near the University. I found a GP near my home who referred me to a Paediatrician. He diagnosed Vestibular dysfunction caused by the forceps delivery. A treatment plan with physiotherapists followed with great improvement in her balance. My daughter had suffered stigma because of her disability so my GP arranged for social counselling for myself and my daughter. I was stressed due to my ex-husband's behaviour and my daughter's health. When I was faced with Court proceedings I was encouraged by my mother and lawyer to accept access by my daughter's father thereby avoiding legal proceedings for custody. I arranged to visit him with my daughter. We went to his home and met with his new wife and their three year old daughter. During the visit the three year old came out of the bathroom and said daddy and I had a shower. He does funny tricks with the soap. Old fears resurfaced. I refused further contact. My ex contacted my lecturers and told them I was an unfit person to be a lawyer. My daughter wanted to have contact with her sister and her father. My mother feared I would never be free of him while I had his child. I was overwhelmed. I took her to his house in tears and left her there. The worst week of my life ensued. It was a repeat of when he had taken her from my arms when she was six months old. He refused to continue her therapy. He said her problems were my fault. After a week my ex returned her to me. He increased the maintenance being paid from $10 per week to $20 per week and he paid the overdue maintenance. I hadn't known my ex-husband's wife was away during the time my daughter stayed with him and his daughter.

I refused further access. He started Court proceedings for my breach of a Court order. A welfare report was conducted by the Family Court. The Court said he could have access but he was not allowed to shower with my daughter. I refused access. He commenced Court proceedings for breach. He told the Judge that he wanted me 'jailed'. He created drama during the proceedings. He was acting on his own behalf. The Courtroom had to be cleared at one point due to his violent behaviour. He had cross examined me endlessly until he was stopped. He dragged it on for three days. On the day of the decision the Judge told him he had had his day in Court in fact he'd had more than his one day. The decision was that I would not be going to jail. Access was granted provisionally. Not at his home. Not at my home. A short period of access. There was a ban on him bringing further Court action against me without prior approval of the Court. He chose not to turn up for the designated access. It was upsetting watching my daughter's disappointment when he didn't show. I sought advice about moving. I moved us to Canberra to complete my Law Degree at ANU.

Removal of my ex from my life allowed me to lead a more productive life. I became a Senior Associate in a large legal firm in Canberra. I opened my own legal practice. When my daughter was thirteen she had contact with her half sister, her father and step mother.

My ex husband passed away in 2000. My daughter had had contact with him whilst she lived in the US. She had maintained a relationship with her father half sister and stepmother. She came home with her husband and son when told her father was in hospital close to death. I drove them to Sydney and we stayed in her father's home. He had been living alone. His marriage to his second wife had ended when their daughter turned sixteen.

I remember that night and the following day. I did not want to stay in my ex's house or visit him at his death bed. My daughter wanted me to 'have closure' I slept in a single bed in a spare bedroom in his house under the orange blankets that were wedding gifts on our marriage all those years before. In the morning we were going to the hospital. At the front door of his home there was a Camellia bush. One flower remained on the bush. I picked it. I took it with me to the hospital. The second wife and child were in the waiting room. My daughter insisted I go to see my ex. Gripping the flower I entered the room. My ex lay there with various tubes. His skin was like rice paper. His eyes were closed. He was no longer the bully. I lent down and left the flower near his cheek. I whispered in his ear 'I am remembering the day you picked Camellias from our garden and took them to the Church on our wedding day. You said in your speech at the reception that you had searched on that morning thinking there weren't any but you looked closer and found some.' It was a message for me that day. He had found me. He loved me. But only as a possession.

The day after his death was strange. I felt a great weight lift from my shoulders. I had always thought I would never live without him in the world. I had outlived him.

I did not attend the funeral. My daughter did. She and her husband rushed to tell me what happened. The couple who had looked after my daughter after her father had run away with her when she was a baby had approached her. They told her not to believe the terrible things her father told her about me. They said I was a lovely young woman. I was not consoled. I recalled my ex had required that I get a psychiatric report that I was fit to look after my daughter before handing her back. I got the report. The Psychiatrist wrote it was in the best interests of the child and the mother that she be returned to the mother. He said to me at the time of his consultation that my husband was the one who required treatment not me. I handed the report to my solicitor. When my husband returned her to me with a potty full of her faeces in a brown paper bag declaring 'you haven't won bitch' I knew the Psychiatrist was right.

Feeling in control of my own destiny I became a Legal Aid panel lawyer assisting women suffering domestic violence and separation matters and as a lawyer and a member of the ACT Law Society council I held a forum to require a Code of Behaviour to protect women in the legal profession in the ACT.

My daughter and her son and husband moved here from the US in 2001. My daughter gave birth to a daughter in 2002. My mother moved to the Sunshine Coast shortly before her death in 2005.

I travelled overseas after my retirement. Two trips to Italy with Writer's groups and a Mediterranean Cruise. I cruised from Amsterdam to Budapest. I had three trips to India one was a Uni Writer's group tour and another was to follow the ancestry trail of my Great grand parents from Britain to India. I travelled through Tasmania doing research for my Thesis. I also travelled to Kenya, Madagascar and Mauritius. When my daughter lived in the US I visited her in New York and San Francisco.

I suffered Deep Vein Thrombosis in 2009 and Pulmonary Embolisms in 2015 and I was diagnosed with an Autoimmune Arthritic Condition following Spinal Surgery in 2017. I curtailed overseas travel in 2018. Once I recovered my health I bought a motor home and I have travelled around Australia.

In 2012 I commenced a Master in Communication (Creative Writing) degree at the Sunshine Coast University. I graduated in 2015.

In 2020 I retired to an Independent Living Unit in Buderim. I have championed causes seeking an end to Elder Abuse and Misogyny including Coercive Control of the elderly. I have sought and received the assistance of the Aged Care Safety and Quality Commission (Qld) on elder abuse matters. I assisted my daughter in a Fair Work claim against her employer. I seek to be the voice for the voiceless the vulnerable and those discriminated against.

My motto: Never give in and never give up serving those in need.

At this point in my life, I seek peace, and a calm journey home to those who went before me and who wait for me.

YELLOW AND BLACK BUTTERFLIES

Richard Dawkins in his book *An Appetite for Wonder* wrote, as a boy, he collected butterflies 'mostly yellow and black swallowtails'. He realised later 'they were probably various species of the genus Papilio'.

On the day of my mother's death in October 2005 my daughter rang me to tell me her house in Buderim was surrounded by Yellow and Black butterflies. I had to tell her Grandma had passed.

On the way to the Retirement Village at Caloundra with tears in my eyes yellow and black butterflies flew into the windscreen and lodged in the wipers.

The photo above is of one of them.

An Appetite for Wonder, Richard Dawkins.
Black Swan. 2014. Page 37.

www.ingramcontent.com/pod-product-compliance
Lightning Source LLC
Chambersburg PA
CBHW062039290426
44109CB00026B/2677